HR at Your Service

Lessons from Benchmark Service Organizations

GARY P. LATHAM AND ROBERT C. FORD

HR at Your Service

Lessons from Benchmark Service Organizations

Society for Human Resource Management

Alexandria, Virginia

www.shrm.org

Strategic Human Resource Management India

Mumbai, India

www.shrmindia.org

Society for Human Resource Management

Haidian District Beijing, China

www.shrm.org/cn

This book is published by the Society for Human Resource Management (SHRM®). The interpretations, conclusions, and recommendations in this book are those of the authors and do not necessarily represent those of the publisher.

The Society for Human Resource Management (SHRM) is the world's largest association devoted to human resource management. Representing more than 250,000 members in over 140 countries, the Society serves the needs of HR professionals and advances the interests of the HR profession. Founded in 1948, SHRM has more than 575 affiliated chapters within the United States and subsidiary offices in China and India. Visit SHRM Online at www.shrm.org.

Interior and Cover Design: Shirley E.M. Raybuck

Library of Congress Cataloging-in-Publication Data

Latham, Gary P.
   HR at your service : lessons from benchmark service organizations / Gary P. Latham and Robert C. Ford.
        p. cm.
   Includes bibliographical references and index.
   ISBN 978-1-58644-247-7
   1. Personnel management. 2. Service industries—Management. 3. Customer relations. I. Ford, Robert C. II. Title.
   HF5549.L2844 2012
   658.3--dc23
                              2011045465
                                              11-0459

Contents

Foreword

This book offers HR managers a new, straightforward way for the HR department to be, and to be seen as, a leader in your organization by applying key concepts from the service/hospitality industry. Best-in-class service providers have learned to hyperfocus on client needs, wants, and expectations — a lesson that seasoned HR executives have learned to apply in their own organizations. This book offers an essential guide to incorporating client-centric service principles in HR management for those who aspire to be HR leaders in their organization. The book is full of contemporary illustrations from the service industry, especially the Walt Disney Company, Marriott International Inc. and The Ritz-Carlton, as well as other top service providers including past and present members of SHRM's Board of Directors.

Drs. Gary Latham and Robert (Bob) Ford are eminently qualified to explain the application of service industry principles to HR management. Gary is the recipient of both the Michael Losey award from the Society for Human Resource Management (SHRM) and the Herbert Heneman award from the Academy of Management's Human Resources Division for lifetime achievement in research that has made a significant contribution to the practice of HR management. He is a Past President of the Society for Industrial and Organizational Psychology as well as the Canadian Psychological Association. He is the President-elect of the International Association for Applied Psychology's Division 1,

Work and Organizational Psychology. He has been awarded the status of Fellow in each of these professional organizations. Gary currently serves on the SHRM Board of Directors, where he chairs the Governance Committee.

Bob is a former editor of the Academy of Management *Executive* and a recipient of the Distinguished Service Award from the Management Education and Development division of the Academy of Management. He is Past President of the Southern Management Association (SMA) and was awarded the status of SMA Fellow and the SMA Distinguished Service Award. He is widely recognized for his published work describing his in-depth knowledge of how successful organizations manage the guest experience in service and hospitality organizations. These two authors have written this book to show how combining their two "worlds" — putting service principles to work in HR — can transform HR management.

—Jose A. Berrios
   President
   BTG: The Berrios Talent Group, LLC
   Chairman
   Board of Directors
   Society for Human Resource Management

Acknowledgements

The authors would like to thank the following people who contributed to this book in many ways. We especially wish to express our appreciation to the members of the Board for the Society for Human Resource Management for their help and encouragement in writing this book. Others who shared stories or offered helpful suggestions for the book are also recognized below. The contributions of all are gratefully acknowledged.

SHRM Board Members

- » Chair Jose A. Berrios, President, Berrios Group, LLC
- » Director-at-Large Melvin L. Asbury, SPHR, President, Asbury Consulting, LLC & SVP, The HR Group, Inc.
- » Director-at-Large Jeffrey M. Cava, EVP, Chief Human Resources Officer, Starwood Hotels & Resorts Worldwide, Inc.
- » Director-at-Large Calvin W. Finch, CPA, Senior Vice President & Chief Financial Officer, CPP, Inc.
- » Director-at-Large Bette J. Francis, SPHR, Vice President/Director of Human Resources, Wilmington Trust Wealth Advisory Services
- » Director-at-Large Carolyn Gould, SPHR, GPHR, CCP, Principal, Global Compliance Services, Pricewaterhouse-Coopers, LLC

» Former Director-at-Large Steven A. Jarrett, Senior Vice President, Human Resources, Financial Industry Regulatory Authority

» Director-at-Large James A. Kaitz, President & CEO, Association for Financial Professionals

» Director-at-Large Virda M. Rhem, SPHR, Directors of Human Resources, Texas Property and Casualty Insurance Guarantee Association

» Former Director-at-Large Gabrielle Toledano, Executive Vice President, Human Resources, Electronic Arts, Inc.

» Director-at-Large Robb E. Van Cleave, SPHR, IPMA-CP, Chief Talent and Strategy Officer, Columbia Gorge Community College, and former chair, SHRM's Board of Directors

Others who contributed to this book:

» Rick Frost, CEO, Louisiana Pacific Corporation

» George Koenig, Senior HR VP, Sodexo Educational Services (retired)

» Soosan Latham, Professor, York University, former Vice President, Human Resource Management, JP Morgan Chase, Toronto

» Gary Parafinczuk, Executive Vice President Corporate Human Resources, formally Stora Enso, currently Tube City IMS

» Janet N. Parker SPHR, Executive Vice President, Corporate HR, Regions Financial Corporation; Former Chair, SHRM's Board of Directors

» Jim Taylor, Vice President, Human Resources, North Pacific Paper Company

And we especially wish to thank our respective wives, Barbara Ford and Soosan Latham, for their ongoing support and willingness to listen to us discuss this book and what it can mean for HRM endlessly. Finally, we want to thank Classical High School for bringing us together in the amazing 1960s.

Chapter 1.

Client-Centric Strategy: A Blueprint for Human Resource Managers

"Give the people everything you can give them."
—Walt Disney, founder, Walt Disney Company

Researchers who study human resource management have documented that HR practices are leading indicators of a firm's financial performance. Yet, many human resource departments are frustrated by the lack of recognition and appreciation they receive for the contributions made to their organization's effectiveness. Further, HR managers have long wondered how they can offer input into crucial decisions and demonstrate how the services they provide can contribute to the organization's overall effectiveness, efficiency, and return on investment (ROI). They long for the opportunity to lead the future thinking on HR management in their organizations instead of defending the value they add from constant cost-cutting initiatives led by those who will not or cannot see what HR contributes to organizational success. The key to gaining participation and defending the value of HR's contributions lies in taking a client-centric approach to delivering HR's services.

Fortunately, the service/hospitality industry provides a blueprint for how HR can remodel itself into a service-oriented department focused on the needs of the managers and employees it serves. Fundamentally, HR is a service department within the organization in which it operates. As such, there are lessons it can learn from benchmark service organizations such as the Walt Disney Co., hotelier Marriott International Inc., Darden's restaurants, and USAA, a provider of financial services to members of the armed forces and their families, among others. Service industry strategies applied by HR managers can transform an HR department by improving its perception by the organization's managers as a department of value-adding leaders, increasing the importance of its voice in the C-suite, and broadening appreciation for and recognition of its invaluable contributions to an organization's success.

Client-centric HR service, informed by the lessons learned in the service industry, provides a straightforward path to improving HR's ability to contribute to an organization's success and to that of its units. Client-centric service is based on two simple steps practiced by successful benchmark service organizations. First, find out what managers and their employees need, want, and expect to be successful, and establish what they are capable of doing. Second, endeavor to meet or exceed their needs, wants, and expectations while enhancing their capabilities.

Although these steps sound simple to do, they are admittedly hard work. Doing what you want to do and know how to do is much easier than asking or studying clients to find out what they really need in order for them to be effective. It is always tempting to take time to solve HR's problems rather than the problems within other departments. That is the traditional way things get done in nonservice organizations, and it is wrong. What HR can learn from Disney, Marriott, Darden, USAA, and many other outstanding service organizations highlighted throughout this book is to find out from clients what is important, valued, and useful — and then act on that knowledge. These service organizations offer HR clear lessons on how to learn from its clients in order to identify, design, and deliver what they truly want, need, and expect human resources to do to find and help solve organizational problems and improve everyone's performance.

The first cardinal lesson to be learned from the service industry is to always start with the customer. Disney invented the term "guestology" to emphasize the company's commitment to its customers, defining it as "the scientific study of a guest's needs, wants, and behaviors."[1] The way for an HR manager to become a respected, recognized leader in the workplace is to do the same for managers and employees: study the client's needs, wants, and behaviors. The opposite approach is patiently sitting in an office and smiling pleasantly when someone asks an HR-related question or requests an HR service. Service is different than servitude, and the best client-centric service is not passive but proactive. HR must seek out how it can co-create solutions with all parts of the organization, even when other departments do not know how to articulate their HR needs. Regardless of what else you do as an HR manager, systematically discovering what the organization's managers and their employees need to be effective is critical to your department's ability to deliver service. When you know what your clients need, you can manage everything and everyone in your department to fulfill those expectations.

The typical human resource management (HRM) graduate-level curriculum emphasizes strategic planning, staffing, performance management, training, labor economics, industrial relations, organizational behavior, legal compliance, compensation plans, information systems, fringe benefits, and the like. What is missing in these academic programs is how to manage human resources in such a way that HR managers will be viewed by everyone else in the organization as "client-centric" enablers rather than as "watchdog" bureaucrats.

The purpose of this book is to explain ways that you — as an HR manager — can ensure that your team develops a strong appreciation for the power of anticipating and attending to the needs, wants, and expectations of managers and their employees first and foremost. Unfortunately, many HR departments lack knowledge of techniques for providing clients with true client-centric service. This lack of knowledge explains the failure of many HR departments in providing value-added services to help managers achieve their respective goals and the mission of the entire organization. Saying "we serve our clients" is one thing, but as you will soon see, benchmark service organizations make this commitment *real* in everything they say and do. Service-oriented HR departments know what makes them valuable in the eyes of all other managers and their employees. They take the time to learn what their clients need, want, and expect from them in order for their clients to be successful. They then demonstrate that their solutions to HR challenges are cost-effective, making HR's service meaningful and memorable. Knowing the behavior and actions that make a service encounter with HR memorable for a manager is what differentiates the HR department that has influence in crucial decisions from one that is merely "there" in the organization.

George Koenig, former Senior HR Vice President for Sodexo Education Food Services, tells how one HR department at an organization in the food service industry established talent benchmarks for employees against which their talents could be measured and assessed, so managers could see instantly where employees they managed ranked in their preparation for other jobs. Appropriate training and career guidance could then be initiated for future job match and success. Since the results of training sessions were connected to the unit's profitability and productivity in quantitative measures, line managers were able to see the value of the training to their own success and to that of the organization. Rather than providing a list of training programs for whatever purpose the manager wished to make of them, the HR department established for those managers the connection between the training offered and the results available in profit terms the managers could readily see and understand.

Client-centric service strategy can elevate HR departments across industries and sectors. Jim Taylor, former Vice President of HR for newsprint maker North Pacific Paper Corp. (NORPAC), jointly owned by Weyerhaeuser Co. and Nippon Paper Industries, made the following observation:

> "In a continuous process industry or 24/7 type of business, it is essential for HR to be responsive at any hour to the needs of line managers. If an employee is injured on the job at 3 a.m. and has to go to the hospital, an HR staff member showing up at the hospital to help the line manager and the employee's family deal with the insurance and communications issues can make for a memorable experience for the family and line manager. That care doesn't have to be limited to on-the-job injuries, either. Showing up for serious injuries that occur outside the workplace can also be highly impactful for showing that the company 'is there' for the people it employs."

NORPAC's HR department believes memorable service encounters can be made in many ways. Become the line manager's "right hand" when dealing with pressing employee issues. Whether the situation involves dealing with a problem employee, supporting a team-building session, or facilitating conflict resolution, you as an HR staff member provide a valuable service to the line manager by being an engaged and active partner in the process. For example, a service-centric HR department in the manufacturing sector helped its production managers also see the value of becoming service centric by designing a process for including customer feedback on product quality, thereby increasing the production managers' appreciation for how tying a service to the physical product added value to the product and profit to the company. By co-producing this process with production, the company benefits from this department's new appreciation for client-centric service taught by a client-centric HR department.

Hallmarks of Service

Today's economy is dominated by service organizations. The U.S. service sector represents between 75 percent and 80 percent of the economy — and its share keeps growing. Even businesses dealing primarily in physical goods now view themselves primarily as service organizations, the physical product being a vital part of the overall service experience, rather than the service being merely an augmentation of the end product. These firms have adopted customer relationships and customer satisfaction as essential metrics for evaluating their effectiveness. Federal Express serves as an example as it defines its delivery service not only in terms of what it offers or provides but as "all actions and reactions that customers perceive they have purchased."

From a neighborhood restaurant to a global chain of resort hotels, from a local auto dealer to a regional utility, and from the IT department to HR, the principles of managing an entire organization or a single department with an emphasis on client-centric service are the same. The benchmark service organizations offer hallmarks for all who believe that their effectiveness depends on their ability to deliver a high-quality and valued service experience to their customers regardless of their industry or product. This philosophy is how they transform themselves from organizations executing exchange relationships with customers to organizations building relationships that matter.

Adding a client-centric approach to executing traditional HR management practices will require most HR departments to learn how to do new things in new ways. Change is never easy. HR has long held the responsibility for designing staffing plans, compensation policies, and performance management systems. These tasks take on a more complex dimension in client-centric HR departments because service is intangible. It exists only in the client's memory as an experience. Although service is an ethereal concept, people know good service when they experience it. This service orientation

P.O. #: 100064232

Ship Via: UPS Ground

Terms:

Bill To:
LYNN GUCK
DFCU FINANCIAL
400 TOWN CENTER DRIVE
DEARBORN, MI 48126
(313) 3228232
LYNN.GUCK@DFCUFINANCIAL.COM

Ship To #: 04812856

Ship To:
LYNN GUCK
DFCU FINANCIAL
400 TOWN CENTER DRIVE
DEARBORN, MI 48126
(313) 3228232
anne.morgan@dfcufinancial.com

UPS Ground

32760563.00025

QTY ORD	BACK ORDER	QTY SHP	ITEM #	LOCATION	DESCRIPTION	LIST PRICE	DISC. PRICE	EXT. PRICE
					Promote the Profession Sale			
					Find huge savings throughout the SHRMStore on HR logo apparel and accessories.			
					Show your HR pride with a new HR shirt, mug, pen or desk accessory and take advantage of great lower-than-ever prices.			
					Visit shrmstore@shrm.org today to make your purchase. But hurry! Supplies are limited.			
1		1 EA	61-15017	BK13A	HR at Your Service: Lessons from Benchmark Service	23.95	23.95	23.95
1	B		48-98029	BM10B	Nine Minutes on Monday: The Quick and Easy Way to Turn	22.00	22.00	22.00
					Above Item is backordered and will ship when available			
1		1 EA	48-22514-2	BL07B	Aligning Human Resources and Business Strategy	40.95	40.95	40.95
			FREIGHT		Freight			11.25
			PAYMENT RECEIVED		Payment Received @ HQ			98.15
					*** THIS IS A PACKING SLIP ONLY. PLEASE DO NOT PAY FROM THIS DOCUMENT. ***			

Total MDSE	Shipping & Handling	Sub-Total	Sales Tax	Total Invoice	Amount Paid & Other Credits	Total Amount Due
86.90	11.25	98.15	.00	98.15	98.15-	.00

Total Wght: 2.55 LB **# Items Shipped:**

Return Policy: See Reverse Side

Delivery Instructions:

Please tear along dotted line and include with your payment. Please reference your invoice # on your payment.
WSSHRM   12/17/13 19:08:48 Job:PRINTER13R/457817 User:SCHEDULER   18-516659 00025 0812856 Page:00041

REMIT TO:

CUSTOMER #:   04812856
INVOICE DATE:
INVOICE #:   32760563
SALES ORDER #: 25348378 SM
TERMS:
TOTAL AMOUNT DUE:

EXPIRATION DATE: ____ / ____

SIGNATURE

PAYMENT METHOD (Choose one):
☐ CHECK ENCLOSED
☐ PLEASE CHARGE TO MY CREDIT CARD: **CARD TYPE (Circle One): MASTERCARD VISA AMEX**

____ / ____ / ____ / ____

PBDPICDU   WSSHRM   12/17/13 19:08:48 Job:PRINTER13R/457817 User:SCHEDULER   18-516659 00025 0812856 Page:00041

PBDPICDR

Please return your package to the following address via UPS so that it is
insured and you have a tracking number available.

SHRM
Return Door# 6
1650 Bluegrass Lakes Pkwy
Alpharetta, GA 30004

If for any reason you are not satisfied with your purchases from the SHRMStore,
please return the item(s), in reasonable condition, within 15 days of receipt.
We will replace your purchase or, if you prefer, issue a refund (less shipping
and handling). Items returned after 15 days will be credited at 50% of their
original purchase price. Returns are not accepted after 30 days. We are unable
to accept returns on audiotapes or software. Returns on video products must be
returned to us within 14 days after the order is delivered to your address
in order to qualify for full credit of the purchase price.

Please keep a record of your return tracking information to ensure that your ret
urn is received at our fulfillment center.

The SHRM Store
1650 Bluegrass Lakes Parkway
Alpharetta, GA 30004

1-800-444-5006 Fed TaxId: 34-0948453

SOCIETY FOR HUMAN
RESOURCE MANAGEMENT

Invoice #:   32760563
Customer #:   04812856
Sales Order #:   25348378 SM
Order Date: 12/17/13
Page #:   1
Invoice Date: 12/17/13

is the real HR product. The benefits package, the pay plan, and the evaluation system are just words on paper until HR makes them come alive by energizing clients to use them. While the paper is as tangible as a refrigerator, the way managers feel about HR services and how they use those services is intangible. Even though the physical aspects of a service experience may be carefully orchestrated, benchmark service organizations know that service quality resides in the *whole* experience — not merely in the design of a room, the softness of a bed, or the taste of prepared food.

The same is true for the services provided by Human Resources. HR experiences do not physically exist. Designing and producing a retirement plan that meets the needs, wants, and expectations of an organization's managers and their employees is quite different from writing a well-thought-out policy. This is a key point. Just because someone in HR develops a policy or creates a procedure does not mean that it meets the needs of the different clients who are to use the policy or follow the procedure. A perfect policy from a technical standpoint that no one uses is useless even if it is legally defensible. The clients are the ones who will ultimately decide if the policy or procedure is worthwhile or adds value. The two most important "clients" are the organization and employees. A great retirement plan that employees love is worthless if it does not benefit the long-term survival and effectiveness of the organization. It is also worthless if employees and managers do not find it useful. *A client-centric HR department actively seeks ways to meet stakeholders' needs.*

The service management literature highlights several benchmark organizations. These include Southwest Airlines Co., Marriott, The Ritz-Carlton Hotel Co., retailer Nordstrom Inc., USAA, Darden, Stora Enso, Sodexo, and, of course, Disney. These organizations realized long ago the value to their respective organization of understanding their customers' expectations. Consequently, they manage their businesses around meeting those expectations. Because they study their customers carefully, they know what their customers need, want, and expect and how to provide it to

Service in Action: NORPAC

Jim Taylor, the former manager of human resources at NORPAC in Washington, led a study on the level of 401(k) participation by hourly plant employees. The results showed that the participation level in his department was significantly below the levels in other departments nationwide. Taylor discovered that the reason for the lower participation levels was simply employee ignorance.

The hourly plant employees lacked knowledge and sophistication about investing money. In short, they were afraid to take advantage of the plan.

Taylor said the following:

We decided to develop an educational session of the 401(k) for all the employees in that department. Once those employees understood how the company was contributing to the plan — really free money

them. The "magic" of Disney is that it not only meets customer expectations but exceeds them in a thousand little ways to get their guests to repeatedly say, "Wow!" Disney achieves this response by studying its guests.

Client-Centric Concepts

Two fundamental concepts in the service industry ensure customer satisfaction. These concepts should be used by HR departments seeking to become client-centric.

First, a client-centric HR department's every action should be focused on and directed to the client. Many HR managers *say* they think first about their clients. But their behavior and time allocations may indicate that in reality they give top priority to their own department's needs and requirements. The first fundamental concept in service requires HR managers to manage from the outside in: *Start with the clients.* Study the overall organization, its managers, and its employees endlessly: Learn their language, for them — and how their own contributions were projected to grow over time and how this might allow them to retire earlier than they had planned, the participation levels shot up dramatically. The result was an increase in trust and appreciation for Human Resources. It changed an attitude of being skeptical of HR when we visited that department to one of being welcome. Every time we would take a walk through that department, employees would want to talk about the stock market, what the future looked like for the company's stock, etc. It became an entree for opening all sorts of discussions. It also reduced voluntary turnover by giving employees a stake in the company, and increased their commitment to doing a good job.

embrace their mission and goals, and support their success by knowing what they want, need, value, do, and expect. Focus everyone in HR on figuring out how to do a better job of meeting and exceeding managers' expectations in ways that help them attain the organization's goals and achieve their mission.

The second fundamental concept practiced by hallmark service organizations is *value each and every client.* In client-centric HR departments, HR staff members constantly and consistently show in word and deed that they value each client. Training the HR staff to think of managers and employees as valued clients whom they serve on behalf of the organization makes a difference in how managers and their employees will see the HR department and its value to them. This approach is more than mere "client orientation." It is recognition that the client should be treated with the respect and attention of any honored and valued guest welcomed to a person's home or table. While we will use the terms "guest," "customer," and "client" throughout the remainder of this book, we want to underscore the noticeable difference between being treated as a partner in a commercial transaction — a customer — and being an honored and valued guest. It is more than a term difference. It is an attitude difference that is noticed by clients and matters to them.

Benchmark service organizations such as Disney know the difference, and HR managers in all organizations should too. Failure to consider your organization's employees as honored and valued clients can lead to a number of negative outcomes, ranging from them ignoring HR's advice to — at the extreme — recommending cutting the HR budget or even outsourcing HR management. If managers view HR as unresponsive and impersonal and an outsourced firm can do the same work as the HR department for less cost, why not trade a high-cost, nonservice-oriented department for a less expensive one?

Seeing managers and their employees as valued clients, however, changes everything the HR department does and how it does it. A line manager comes to the HR department seeking to obtain advice on a subject in which HR has expertise. If HR provides a memorable experience by demonstrating a client-centric attitude

---

Service in Action: Stora Enso

The Stora Enso HR department had a cost-effective, centralized approach to delivering HR services. The group was so effective that other companies benchmarked the department. Nevertheless, Stora Enso received constant complaints from support functions, particularly sales and marketing, about HR. The gist was that it was difficult to do business with HR.

Without adding staff, HR resolved the complaints by assigning an existing HR staff member as the sales and marketing business partner. She became the first point of contact on all HR issues. Her helpful attitude and easy availability instantly increased the quality of HR's service delivery to sales and marketing and changed human resources' reputation companywide.

and taking client-centric actions while delivering that advice, the line manager will think "Wow! This HR department is fantastic." Creating an experience that revolves around the client, instead of merely providing a cost-effective service, is a simple way to turn line managers into champions of Human Resources. Doing so requires a genuine willingness to listen to clients, demonstrating a caring attitude that turns an otherwise routine transaction into a client-centric experience that impresses them.

Clearly, exceptional HR departments are already putting the principles of client-centric service to work. At Weyerhaeuser, a forest products company, HR staff members serve as internal consultants to line managers. They (1) coach managers on how to cope with problem employees, (2) help employees appeal denied medical claims, and (3) provide advice on ways to get "relief" from a restrictive company policy without violating the intent of that policy. This kind of personal service creates positive client-centric experiences for line managers and their employees alike. Actions such as these have greatly enhanced HR's stature and effectiveness at Weyerhaeuser.

Looking beyond sales and marketing, the head of HR North America introduced a set of HR metrics to line management that measured HR effectiveness (What results are we getting from our programs?), HR efficiency (How cost-effective is the HR department in delivering HR services?), and HR alignment (Is HR delivering what management has determined as high priority for HR?). These data became part of the fundamental strategic planning process that factored in client needs with the overall business strategy. Line managers in Stora Enso now see HR as critical to attaining the company's overall strategic objectives.

To comprehend the importance of this fundamental concept of client-centric service, think about the organizations with which you interact in your own daily life. To some companies, you are only a face in a commercial transaction; others treat you as a welcomed guest or valued customer. The difference is so clear it is unforgettable. Anyone who has been to a Hyatt Regency hotel knows the special way guests are treated. Your HR staff can and should treat clients in your organization with the care that great hotels treat their guests. Any HR department seeking success in this modern era must learn this basic service lesson: People are increasingly aware of who treats them "right" while solving their problems, delivering expertise, or helping them achieve their goals.

While these two concepts — *focus on the client* and *value each and every client* — sound straightforward, they create challenges that the benchmark organizations in the service industry spend time, energy, and money to meet. The lessons they have learned offer invaluable lessons for HR managers. The purpose of this book is to share these lessons with you.

Strategy, Staff, and Systems

There are three critical S's that client-centric HR departments pay careful attention to: strategy, staff, and systems. First is strategy. How must HR define its mission and goals to guide its staff toward performing in a client-centric way? Next is the staff. How do you hire, train, and reward your HR staff so that everyone delivers the high-quality experience that every client expects every time? This consistency of commitment is what distinguishes a client-centric HR department. Lastly are systems. How do you make certain that a service-oriented HR department has an effective array of systems to deliver the service that managers and their employees need to be successful in reaching their goals? The service industry's hallmarks know that an impressive statement of customer commitment in a mission statement and a big smile by an employee cannot make up for burned lasagna, a dirty hotel room, a late airline flight, or a broken air conditioner. Likewise, good intentions cannot overcome a faulty HR system or an HR staff member's indifference to an employee's wants, a manager's needs, or organizational performance expectations.

A service organization's strategy, staff, and systems are obviously related to each other. They all have one focus — the client — and all three exist for one overriding purpose: to achieve the mission of providing client satisfaction that results in organizational effectiveness. The same should be true for HR as it focuses on its clients.

Table 1.1 captures the principal aspects of developing a service-centric strategy for your HR department.

Table 1.1

Client-Centric HR Strategy
1. Define, create and sustain a total client-centric service culture within HR.
2. Align HR strategy with the key drivers of your organization's strategy.
3. Identify and provide the HR services that managers and their employees need, want, and expect in order to attain their strategic goals and the overall organizational mission.

Client-Centric HR Staffing
1. Hire HR staff who love to serve clients.
2. Train your HR staff to provide client-centric services.
3. Empower your HR staff to deliver services in a client-centric way.

Client-Centric HR Systems
1. Provide seamless HR service delivery.
2. Pursue service perfection relentlessly.
3. If it breaks, fix it. Don't fail managers or their employees twice.
4. Lead HR staff to service excellence.

Provide the Best Choice

Service from HR departments is too often perceived by clients as unsatisfactory. Dissatisfied line managers will both avoid and denigrate the HR department. Consequently, they seek ways to cut

HR out of the loop. The way to prove your department's commitment to the organization lies in offering to co-create with clients the best solutions for them to get their tasks done and goals accomplished. Co-creating solutions with clients requires stellar client-centric service such as that delivered by the Norpac, Stora Enso, and Weyerhaeuser HR departments, depicted in our earlier examples.

Managers in the service industry know that if they want customers to keep coming back to their hotel, restaurant, retail store, or insurance company, instead of going elsewhere, they must confirm that everyone who works for them know what excellent service is and how to provide it to customers. If customers are disappointed by unsatisfactory service from one organization, they know they can probably find a similar organization just down the street, and they will not hesitate to go there. If an HR department wants its clients to look to it for expertise in reaching their performance goals, HR too must provide excellent service.

Service in Action: Walt Disney World Resort

The Walt Disney World Resort in Orlando, Florida, provides an exceptionally wide representation of best practices in the hospitality industry. Across the resort's 43-square-mile property are successful examples of restaurants ranging from quick-serve to fine dining; lodging from campgrounds to upscale hotels; a transportation system including trains, boats, buses, and monorails; retail stores; golf courses; and (not far away) cruise ships.

Disney has been a pioneer in providing outstanding customer experiences in at least three key ways. First, Disney uses themes to help make the service environment consistent with the expectations of its guests. For example, the Magic Kingdom is based on the fantasy themes of the beloved Disney characters, who are seen everywhere,

HR clients who feel they are receiving unsatisfactory expertise will find ways to avoid using HR in the future. They will see HR as the "organizational cop" instead of the HR problem-solver. Moreover, they will exclude HR when it is time to bring together the team that defines the organizational mission, sets the performance goals, and makes the strategic decisions to attain them. More ominously, they will also look for ways to cut costs — including the possibility of outsourcing HR activities and functions. If you cannot show you add value by being in the organization, you probably are not adding value, and you will probably not stay long.

Now that it's clear that becoming service-oriented can add value to your HR department, let us look at the key principles of client-centric service management. Our examples are drawn from some of the world's most successful service organizations. All of these principles can be successfully adapted by HR departments that seek to be client-centric.

suggesting to guests that they are visiting a fantasy world. In doing so, Disney turns a business transaction with its customers into a personal relationship by fostering an emotional connection. Second, Disney learned early that the satisfaction customers derive from their experiences is a direct function of employees' satisfaction in providing those experiences. Disney managers and supervisors know how to achieve and maintain the levels of employee satisfaction that motivate employees to provide outstanding, memorable customer experiences. Third, they have built a culture that teaches and reinforces the organization's values in countless ways to remind employees of what is important to Disney visitors. Disney's careful attention to employee training and its efforts in reinforcing a culture of guest-centric service for both employees and guests contribute to the company's "wow" factor with its staff and visitors.

The Basics of "Wow": HR's Clients Know Best

Among the challenges for client-centric HR departments is to ensure that their staff consistently offer the high level of service that managers and employees want and expect. They must understand the truth that service managers know well: Service quality and service value are defined solely in the mind of the client. While *Consumer Reports* from time to time evaluates an airline, hotel, or restaurant, in HR decisions about the quality and value of an HR department is made anew by each individual client in every transaction with HR.

To create a service-oriented, client-centric department, HR must study its clients to know what they expect, what they need, what their limitations are, and how they get things done. The client experience has three components: the service product, the service setting or environment, and the service delivery. In short, HR strategy, staff, and systems can be aligned to meet or exceed the client's expectations regarding each of these three by systematically studying managers, their employees, and their performance needs and goals. This way, HR leaders can identify what managers need and want from HR, how they want to be treated when they interact with HR, and how to make them satisfied that HR provided the service they wanted — even if they did not know initially how to define their needs.

One such expectation is HR staff's accessibility. Weyerhaeuser, for example, knows that older employees in their hourly workforce are often uncomfortable going to the HR department, especially if the department is not easily accessible (for example, far away from the pulp mill, saw mill, or logging site). Weyerhaeuser does not expect most hourly employees to be comfortable going to the HR department if the office contains expensive furniture and if HR staff members wear dress attire. Weyerhaeuser's HR department knows the significance of going to the employees. Consequently, they visit the worksites regularly. In an effort to remain approachable, they ask questions and listen closely to their clients.

By studying managers, particularly their performance goals and how their operation contributes to the organizational mission, HR will know how to design systems, develop processes, and craft an effective strategy to enable managers to attain major objectives. Studying the managers and their jobs allows HR to co-create with its clients practices that deliver outstanding service to them. "It all starts with the client" is not just an inspirational slogan. In a truly client-centric HR department, it is a standard that everyone in HR must accept and rise to. Building materials manufacturer Louisiana-Pacific Corp. practices this kind of client-centric service. Chief Executive Officer Rick Frost affectionately describes his HR manager as having big ears and a soft touch.

Meeting Client Expectations

Customers come to a service provider with expectations. Just as Olive Garden knows that all customers, new and repeat, expect food of good quality at a fair price, fast and attentive service, and a clean, pleasant atmosphere, HR's clients have expectations too. Timely service, systems that work efficiently and effectively, and a shared commitment to organizational effectiveness are among HR's client expectations. But as an HR manager, you cannot know your client's expectations until you ask. Thus, client-centric HR managers continuously solicit feedback from their clients on how the HR department can meet and exceed their expectations.

An HR manager must understand and plan for these expectations before clients enter the HR department so that they have a positive experience. This preparation should extend to even the simplest things that can impact the client experience with HR. At Disney, for example, the road from the Magic Kingdom's Main Street USA hub to Tomorrowland is wider than the road to Adventureland. Based on previous research, the park's planners anticipated that more people would choose to walk to the right (toward Tomorrowland) at a point where they were indifferent as to which way to go. Disney knew from studying its customers that more people are right-handed, and indifferent people tend to go in the direction of their handedness. Because Disney took the time to observe this pattern, it could plan the width of pathways to better accommodate what it knows guests are likely to do. Has your HR department taken the time to thoroughly understand how clients access HR services and to communicate with HR staff? As Yogi Berra is fond of saying, "You can hear a lot by listening."

In the same way, HR needs to spend the time and effort to understand what its clients say they need, want, and expect from the HR department and how HR leaders actually manage human

Service in Action: The Walt Disney World Resort

Disney learned from asking its guests about expectations that one of the leading drivers for guest satisfaction is cleanliness. Keeping a theme park clean is not only essential; it is a big job. In studying customer behavior, Disney learned two things. First, if cast members — the Disney term for park employees — constantly pick up even the smallest bits of trash, park customers tend to dispose of their own trash. When cast members practice and respect cleanliness, the customers emulate them. Second, Disney also learned from studying its guests that people tend to throw their trash into trashcans that are conveniently placed not far apart and are easily seen. Thus, Disney locates its trashcans to match those criteria. Go inside the Magic Kingdom on a quiet day when the crowds are not distracting, and you will see that Main Street USA looks like a forest of trash cans, each located 25 to 27 paces apart. Listening to guests and observing their behavior enabled Disney managers to understand how guests respond to environmental cues. That knowledge helps the managers maintain a high standard of cleanliness.

resources. When the HR department translates this understanding the same way Disney does, into actions and deeds that improve its client service, HR can also achieve a client-centric operation. Stora Enso's HR department studied the needs of line managers and in the process discovered that by assigning an HR staff member to a business unit, that they had transformed HR became a "business partner" in the eyes of Stora Enso's line managers.

The Total Service Experience

If the HR department' goal is to provide an outstanding experience to its clients, then HR must understand why a manager or employee comes to the department, what these people expect, and how HR staff can meet their expectations. Supplying a well-crafted HR policy or legal HR procedure is not enough; the total service experience is what matters. Many people think running a restaurant is relatively simple: Cook good food, and everything else takes care of itself. Client-centric, profitable restaurants know that customers patronize them for many reasons having nothing to do with food quality. Managing the total service experience is a much bigger job than merely executing a good recipe. Client-centric HR management involves systematically determining what those many reasons are, modeling them, measuring their impact on the client experience, testing various strategies that might improve the quality of that experience, and then providing the combination of factors or elements that not only attract clients repeatedly but results in them treating HR as their partner.

HR has extensive contact with line managers and their employees. Client-centric HR managers know that much of their effectiveness is due to their staff members' ability and willingness to see their many clients the same way that Disney or the Ritz-Carlton sees their guests. Consequently, these HR managers spend an inordinate amount of time and effort finding ways to help the staff provide excellent service to the organization's managers and their employees. They know that if they neglect to ensure that their HR staff have the resources, training, and motivation to provide the excellent service needed by the organization's managers and employees, the HR department is likely to fail in the eyes of the client.

The HR department at Darden Restaurants Inc. recognizes that the principles for providing an outstanding service for diners are the same principles that must be applied to Darden's restaurant managers and their employees. Darden HR managers know they must also meet or exceed the expectations of the HR staff regarding how they are treated. People tend to treat others as they are treated by their leaders, to care about what their leaders care about, and to be only as committed as their leaders are to them. Extensive research by organizational psychologist Benjamin Schneider at Valtera supports this conclusion. HR staff should be given the same care and consideration that the HR department expects its staff to extend to line managers and their employees. Southwest Airlines supports this viewpoint. As expressed in a part of Southwest Airline's mission statement, "Employees will be provided the same concern, respect, and caring attitude within the organization that they are expected to share externally with every Southwest Customer."

Going Forward

For businesses big and small, from an international airline to a neighborhood sports bar, surviving and prospering in the present competitive environment requires mastering the principles of service. Human Resources, too, faces increasing numbers of competitors who advertise themselves as doing the same quality job as an organization's HR operation yet faster, cheaper, and more client-focused. HR departments that seek to survive and prosper must master the principles of service. Not only will a client-centric HR department be better able to demonstrate its added value to the organization, it can serve as a role model to other departments in the organization, in much the same way as the Disney cast members picking up trash in the Magic Kingdom model good behavior for park visitors. The HR department should be seen as the exemplar of how to be client-centric and take the leadership in infusing a client-centric orientation across the entire organization.

Charles Revson, founder of cosmetics maker Revlon Inc., drew a distinction between what his organization makes and what the clientele buys: "In the factory we make cosmetics. In the store we sell hope." What does the HR department provide in the eyes of its clients? How effective is your HR staff in supporting and empowering a manager who must maneuver through a maze of laws and regulations that affect line managers' ability to make a better product or to deliver a better service than competitors? Does your HR department instill hope, helping clients believe they can achieve their goals?

The HR department must unshackle itself from the role of "police officer" in the organization. HR staff members can increase their perceived value in the eyes of line managers and their employees if they act as internal consultants who are known for helping clients achieve goals that in turn lead to organizational success. They can help by making their expertise available to clients in all aspects of human resources, including goal setting, strategic planning for goal attainment, training to teach employees how to achieve the goals, performance management, and coaching techniques for motivating employees to use their abilities to execute strategy. HR manages the most important resource in an organization. HR's value to managers across the organization lies in its ability to help them effectively manage human capital — enabling the organization to succeed.

Chapter Takeaways

1. Start with the clients: the HR department's every action should be focused on and directed to its clients.

2. Treat every HR client with the same care that service organizations treat their customers.

3. Invent ways to meet all key stakeholders' needs at the same time, with an eye on the overall organization's goals and strategy for attaining them.

4. Remember that the client determines the quality and value of HR service.

5. Seek feedback from clients on how HR can meet and exceed their expectations, and act on that feedback to improve service delivery to them.

Chapter 2.

Providing Client-Centric Service: Delivering Quality Clients Value

"Listen to your customers. They'll tell you what to do."
— Norman Brinker, founder, Brinker International

When Gary Parafinczuk arrived in London as head of the corporate HR department for Stora Enso, the global paper, packaging, and wood products company, his number one project was to establish an "HR shared service" organization for Finland, Sweden, and Germany. As is true for many other similarly sized companies, Stora Enso's executive management wanted an improvement in HR service at a lower cost. With 27,000 employees and 88 production facilities in more than 35 countries, centralizing and improving HR service was no easy feat. The project had been going on for more than a year with no real progress. The problem, Parafinczuk discovered upon his arrival, was rather obvious to him in hindsight:

> "There was no clear picture at the time of what the HR vision and platform should look like let alone what it should cost. HR lacked the data necessary to identify the best possible solution. HR also lacked alignment across the organization as to what model would best fit the needs of Stora Enso. There was no clear mandate from senior management to 'move forward.'"

Parafinczuk knew that providing superior value to HR's clients throughout the organization meant understanding executive management's requirements as well as HR best practices for organizations of similar size and type. So he tested various approaches in terms of service and cost that would align with and support the company's business strategy. Ultimately, the solution was not an "HR shared services" organization but a whole new "HR service delivery model."

After receiving the mandate from top management to install the new "HR Service Delivery Model," Stora Enso's HR department developed a straightforward vision statement to nail down its approach in terms of service level, cost, and quality. The department articulated its mission in the following statement: "To achieve the required service level at the lowest possible costs." This process led to a comprehensive presentation to senior management so top executives could see what was possible at what cost — and what the tradeoffs would be at each level. Then, together they were able to make informed choices about the tradeoffs involved.

When line managers and other staff (for example, marketing, finance, R&D, and logistics) come to the HR department for assistance, they want certain things to happen. They may want sound, timely advice; a smooth hiring process; an enticing, functional benefits package; or creative solutions to employee grievances — whatever their expectations, they want them to be fully met. Line managers and other staff will support HR only if their experiences meet or exceed their expectations of how HR should help them succeed in achieving their performance goals.

Three Service Strategies Adaptable to HR

McDonald's gives its customers speed and low prices. The Four Seasons' restaurant provides diners with superior quality. Harvard University professor and business strategist Michael Porter breaks strategies into three categories: low cost, differentiation, and filling a market niche. McDonald's opts for the low-cost approach; Four Seasons differentiates itself with high quality. As is true for any service organization, no HR department can do it all. The HR department must determine the basis on which it will best serve the organization.

An HR department, with a service mindset, can employ one or more of these three different generic strategies. First, it can aim to provide cost leadership by being a low-cost provider. Second, it can differentiate its service from other providers of HR services (for example, those inside and outside the organization) with high-quality, in-house service. Third, it can find an HR niche on which to focus and then outsource all other HR functions. (This strategy can be seen where HR concentrates on value-added services that require unique expertise and contracts with external providers to perform routine HR functions.) Client-centric organizations establish a strategy that includes one or more of these approaches, and then they stick with it. An HR department' primary strategic choice centers on what HR mission best supports the overall organizational strategy. Does the business strategy require a low-cost, transactional, compliance-focused HR function? Or does it require a value-added, transformational, development-focused HR niche? These are strategic choices. HR must make these strategic choices based on how it sees its role and mission supporting the overall organization's strategy.

Low Cost vs. High Competence

"We will minimize costs!" is the approach some companies adopt. Southwest Airlines focuses on reducing the costs of running the airline (for example, turnaround times, loading and unloading, food service, and more) to achieve the lowest production cost per mile in the industry. Wal-Mart focuses on controlling inventory and cutting merchandise costs through mass buying. These two low-price producers offer excellent service at a price so low that competitors cannot offer the same service and value at a lower price without going broke.

However, an HR department employing this strategy must be cautious. By reducing costs to be a low-price service provider, any resulting deterioration in service may decrease the value that clients receive from HR, leading to calls for all or part of HR operations to be outsourced. HR staff must continuously ask two critical questions: (1) Why do we exist? (2) Who would miss us if we were gone? Answering these questions means that HR should never fear investing in improving HR services and processes as long as it is prepared to defend the return on investment the organization gets from those investments.

To answer these questions, HR staff need data — employee surveys, internal client satisfaction surveys, organizational assessments, and the like — to understand precisely what services, and what level of those services it needs to provide and how well clients perceive the staff is providing them currently. Armed with data, HR managers can then engage senior management in a strategic discussion on the HR department's mission and on how HR service should be provided. For some organizations with low-cost strategies, this approach may translate into minimum HR service. For other organizations that need sophisticated services and organizational functionality, greater HR expertise and service is required. In the end, an organization's business model and strategy determine the level of HR service needed for the organization.

Differentiating the HR Product

All service organizations practice product differentiation. Many focus on attracting clients by emphasizing these differences rather than by trying to operate on a bare-bones budget. Thus, an airline might advertise the quality of its flying experience rather than only focusing on price to differentiate itself from Southwest Airlines.

An HR department can differentiate itself by communicating to managers and their employees about the value of its services: how HR will improve their ability to attain their goals, how HR matters to the success of the organization, and how it can provide greater value relative to what other budget expenditures yield for the organization. As Yogi Berra would say, "Making a difference makes a difference." In an era of movies filled with sex and violence, all of us are familiar with the "difference" in Disney movies. Disney provides wholesome, family entertainment, which matters to and is valued by its customers. Hotels try to differentiate themselves in the marketplace by advertising special amenities ("Free continental breakfast!" "Kids sleep free!"). The Holiday Inn Family Suites Resort in Lake Buena Vista, Florida, sets itself apart from other hotels by offering only suites, including Kidsuites with rooms themed for children; Sweetheart Suites for romantics; Cinema Suites with separate theater rooms featuring large-screen televisions with state-of-the-art stereo systems and dual recliners for film lovers; and Fitness Suites with Nautilus equipment with separate workout rooms for those who relish a private workout.

Another way to differentiate HR's service is through a strong brand image. Creating a strong brand will extend the HR department's reach to other departments. This brand has to be earned and, hence, does not come quickly. Creating the HR brand comprises at least three essential elements:

1. How HR helps the organization offer employees an attractive career path,
2. How it designs an effective reward package in terms of compensation and benefits to attract and retain employees, and
3. How it creates ways to accelerate the implementation and internalization of the organization's strategy within employees.

Branding in these three areas is particularly significant because building a brand means creating trust with existing and new employees as well as with the senior management team. And in today's environment, organizations need their employees to trust the HR brand so that when, for example, organizations must make necessary changes in the strategy or benefits package, they do not lose the confidence and support of their current employees or discourage potential recruits. One organization, Gaylord Hotels, was so committed to establishing its brand as a trusted employer that it created an employee guarantee similar to its customer guarantee that offered to redress situations in which customers feel they have in some way been failed by the company. Employees at Gaylord are told what Gaylord will guarantee them in the employment relationship upon hiring, and they are encouraged to exercise their right of redress if they think that guarantee has been violated in any way. This service has won Gaylord numerous "employer of choice" awards, the trust of its employees, and a highly qualified candidate pool. Its brand as an employer makes the difference.

The Disney name instantly communicates wholesome value to the customer on whatever it appears. A carefully managed brand image similarly enables McDonald's and Marriott to quickly gain acceptance for anything new they bring into the marketplace. Customers give the new product or service a try on the basis of the brand's reputation. Thousands of people, many of them families who had never before felt comfortable going on a cruise, booked trips on the Disney Magic even before the new cruise service was launched. They knew that Disney would not risk its brand on a venture inconsistent with customer expectations of what Disney represents. What brand image does your HR department have in your organization? What are the expectations of clients when HR introduces new products or procedures to your organization? The answer is likely to be positive if your HR staff have earned a reputation for trustworthiness by practicing a genuine, client-centric service orientation in its attitude and actions.

In what ways can the quality of service provided by your HR department be shown to be superior to the services provided by other staff departments in your organization that are competing for the same dollars? How is your HR department superior to an outsourced organization that claims to give the same service for less cost? In today's cost-conscious environment, the answer cannot be vague. If the value difference cannot be demonstrated in terms everyone can see and understand, the provider is at risk. Managers are unlikely to support an HR department that cannot clearly show its value to the organization and its operating units.

One way to show how the HR department makes a difference is to provide measures on how HR has helped energize employees to internalize and accelerate the implementation of their organization's strategic plan. As the saying goes, "That which gets measured gets done." HR needs to manage its function like any other part of the business — with data. This means having an appropriate human resources information system (HRIS), including relevant, credible internal customer surveys. When HR provides client-centric service, the benefits to the organization should be proven by the data collected.

At Stora Enso, HR for North America conducts an annual comprehensive internal customer survey of the top 200 managers in the division. It solicits opinions on HR's service platform, including talent management, compensation and benefits, organizational development, employee and labor relations, HR administration, and safety. This material, along with the results of an annual employee survey, is reviewed with senior management and then used to formulate the HR department's annual objectives and the strategy to attain them.

While the client ultimately determines which HR services matter most, HR managers need to be, and to be seen as, the ones who co-create with clients solutions to problems, making clients and the overall organization more effective. Whether by offering expert advice on ways line managers can select and coach their best performers to gain the commitment of the rest of their team to attain specific high goals, or by being an internal consulting agency for line and staff managers, an HR department must prove it makes a difference with high-quality service metrics on an ongoing basis.

Creating a Niche

The third strategy that can be used separately or in combination with the previous two is filling a niche. Besides being cost-effective and differentiating itself from other options, an HR department can find a unique niche that enables it to stand out in ways that the organization will both recognize and appreciate. As an Italian restaurant might elect to create a niche by concentrating on northern Italian cuisine, or a hotel might create a niche by concentrating on features that attract high-end conventions, an HR department too can identify a niche that will serve the organization in specific and meaningful ways. This method can be especially helpful in organizations where HR issues have not historically been part of the strategic planning process, since it can establish the value of HR's contributions to the strategic issues impacting the human capital of the organization — arguably its greatest asset.

An HR department can also carve a niche for itself by focusing on reliability, responsiveness, and client empathy. Each of these can be achieved through proximity, both physically and figuratively, to clients. Lack of any one of these characteristics will hurt an HR department that desires a reputation for being client-centric. As noted in Chapter 1, having an HR office physically close to and convenient for hourly workers increases the likelihood of them interacting with and opening up to HR staff. When the HR department is in a separate building at a distant location with an intimidating environment (for example, suits and ties, ornate furniture), some workers may be reluctant to approach the staff. Regardless of the physical location, client-centric HR managers direct their staff to make regular rounds of the operating floor, to regularly visit remote locations where employees are working, and to be easily accessible to those who want and need their services. When HR staff make themselves readily available to clients, clients can access HR services while on duty instead of having to come to work early or stay late. On the flip side, HR staff will gain visibility by going to the employees on the operating floor, even at distant work locations, and such service will benefit the department's reputation.

JetBlue Airways, the low-fare, high-frequency, point-to-point carrier, established itself as a quality service provider by promoting more leg room and by being among the first to provide a back-of-the-seat TV. What niche can your HR department fill to win the strong support of your organization? Career counseling might be one; advising ways to obtain work/life balance might be another.

Service in Action: Stora Enso

Gary Parafinczuk knows that identifying an unmet need and filling an untargeted niche can help an HR department bring value to the whole organization. He tells the following story:

During a particularly rough period when I was head of HR for Stora Enso North America, we were going through a major downsizing and a restructuring that included downgrading our benefits package for employees. One of my HR administrators proposed that we organize a "Work/Life Balance Fair" for our office employees. In principle, I was all for it. On a practical level, my first reaction was there would be an overwhelming cynical response from employees, and no one would show up. The HR administrator was so enthusiastic and persistent about this, and had done so much homework to organize it, that I couldn't say no. So, we went ahead and held the program. Work-life experts and vendors set up shop in one of our office buildings. The attendance was very high and the positive employee feedback was almost off the charts. This program has become an annual offering by HR. This all happened because an individual with vision and enthusiasm identified a need that HR could fulfill, and found the right approach to meet it.

Combining Strategies

Successful theme parks combine strategies by advertising a park visit as a high-value, low-cost, family-entertainment experience that is different from any other. At those times of the year when the tourism volume is weak, many Florida theme parks offer Florida residents special discount prices to attract guests from the local market.

An HR department can seek to distinguish itself by positioning its services in clients' minds as the best value for the lowest cost (for example, 401(k) plans or educational opportunities). This combination of strategies requires an HR department to discover and execute efficiencies that allow it to operate at a low cost, while communicating the quality of its service. Some HR departments have differentiated themselves by identifying key areas of concern for their organization's managers, seeking out benchmark exemplars of providers of those vital services, and displaying their performance in comparison to those benchmarks as a way to affirm the value they add to the organization on principal areas that matter.

Establishing a close and trusting relationship with clients will be difficult if HR stresses only low costs. Telling an employee to go to the Internet for answers may be the least expensive way to provide a service. But for people who are technology-challenged or are very busy, such a directive is annoying to say the least. Client-centric HR managers have found that the best way to succeed in the long term is to provide better service and value than other staff departments in the organization, balancing speed, cost, and quality while reinforcing their brand differences or exploiting an unmet niche. They accomplish this goal by knowing their clients' needs, wants, expectations, and capabilities. As Tom Peters, author of *The Circle of Innovation,* wrote, "You can knock off everything … except awesome service." HR staff at Weyerhaeuser have embraced this truism. They are constantly on the shop floor. By going out into operations, they see firsthand the conditions in which their clients work; they know what the line managers and their employees need to do their jobs. They then quickly find ways to co-produce with them ways to meet those needs with high-quality services and products.

Service Encounters and the "Moment of Truth"

Service encounters are crucial to a customer's evaluation of an organization's service quality. They can make or break the entire customer experience. A service encounter occurs at the moment a client interacts with a service provider. Jan Carlzon, the former president of Scandinavian Airlines, a division of SAS Group, refers to the pivotal moments during these interactions as *moments of truth*. For example, a passenger's first interaction with airline personnel is an obvious moment of truth, and that single moment can determine whether the potential passenger leaves your airline and goes to another, or whether a lifetime relationship with the passenger has begun. Carlzon managed the entire airline with a focus on providing good service at each moment of truth, "the 15 golden seconds" during which the mammoth airline is represented by one server to one customer. During the moment of truth in a service encounter with a customer, one mistake made by the provider can taint the overall experience; for the customer the restaurant is no good, the airline inept, and the hotel a major disappointment.

Obviously, if a meal was bad, an airplane did not fly, or the hotel room was not clean, the customer will not care how pleasant the server, flight attendant, or concierge were. On the other hand, since most meals are similar to other meals, most plane rides are like other plane rides, and most hotels get it right, the distinguishing characteristic of most customer experiences is how the people providing the service performed it. Even if the meal, plane ride, or hotel suite are among the best in your life, a rude or careless service provider can ruin your experience in an instant. When that happens, all the organization's other efforts and expenditures have been wasted. This reason is why client-centric HR staff members must identify and manage the moments of truth with their clients effectively.

One unfortunate interaction with HR staff, a missed deadline on a form submission, or an unreturned phone call to a line manager can negatively influence the opinion of HR among your organization's leadership. The success or failure of a client experience with any member of the human resource department often depends on that single moment of truth, and one mistake will likely lead to client complaints about the ineptitude of the HR department. Consequently, HR needs to make sure, as does Scandinavian Airlines, *that every client is recognized by every HR staff member as important in every experience with HR.* No service failure is acceptable. Nonetheless, client-centric HR managers prepare for failures, as failures do occur. Human resource systems inevitably have problems. To not anticipate that someone in HR will one day fail a client is wishful thinking. For more ways to plan to meet client expectations, see Chapter 3.

Characteristics of a Quality Service Encounter

The purchase of an airline ticket is a brief service encounter. The interaction between a customer and an agent at a hotel front desk is usually somewhat longer, and the series of interactions between customer and server in a restaurant is an even longer encounter. A day in a theme park may involve 50 to 100 service encounters. Although many service situations or interactions in HR can be automated — Internet-based ordering systems being a familiar example — the term *service encounter* still refers to the person-to-person interaction or series of interactions between a client and the HR staff member delivering the service.

Gary Parafinczuk from Stora Enso tells the following story: "I had an HR professional working for me who, from a skill point of view and in terms of results, was an average performer. Yet, she consistently received above average customer feedback evaluations from line management. Why? Her relationship skills handling executives and middle managers were outstanding. She was a good listener and she kept in constant communication with her clients. Consequently, even when she sometimes didn't deliver as she should have, they gave her the benefit of the doubt."

This example demonstrates that even when things do not go perfectly, a client-centric staff member who has built a strong relationship with a client can diminish the impact of a service problem. No HR department is perfect. The good will the HR department can build by its commitment to client-centric service can pay off when a failure to provide an expected service occurs. In an HR department that had not made the client-centric effort to build that good will, an employee came to the HR office before going home from the graveyard shift. He had been waiting for 30 minutes because the end of his shift occurred earlier than the start of an HR staff member's. When the HR staff employee arrived, he immediately poured himself a cup of coffee, chatted with other HR staff who were coming through the door, and ignored the tired employee. Little wonder that this employee remains resentful of the HR department for the lack of respect shown to him that day long ago.

Service encounters have specific characteristics. Knowing them can help an HR department ensure that staff members manage their many moments of truth with clients effectively.

Services Are Consumed at the Moment or During the Period of Production

Working to meet client expectations at or during the period of production is a major difference between successful service organizations and unsuccessful ones. Once the service experience happens, it is over. The HR department cannot replace a broken promise, toss a bad customer encounter into a rework pile for fixing later, or correct an out-of-specification service delivery process. If the experience goes badly, the person delivering the service must be the one to fix it. In a client-centric HR department, the focus is on the client experience and empowering the HR staff who serve the clients. Instead of concentrating on control systems, client-centric HR managers empower their staff to take action. Managers are unable to watch every client-HR staff interaction. Consequently, they must enable their HR staff to know how and why the consistent delivery of a high-quality client experience is critical to line managers and their employees, the organization's success, and HR's stature in the organization.

Service Encounters Must Meet Manager and Employee Expectations

If the service that line managers receive from the HR department falls short of what they expected, they will be unhappy. They will remember the events surrounding the poor service HR staff provided. If enough people tell their co-workers what a terrible experience the HR department provided, HR's reputation will be severely tarnished. The challenge for client-centric HR departments is to anticipate their client's expectations of them. As discussed in Chapter 1, client-centric HR leaders spend the extra time necessary to determine client expectations, especially by gathering the requisite data through employee surveys and day-to-day informal communications.

If a cruise line, hotel, or a restaurant cannot meet customers' expectations, it should not promise more than it can deliver. During difficult times for the airlines, no-frills Southwest Airlines continued to do well. One reason is that its superb service is tempered by realistic customer expectations of what the low-cost airline offers. Ed Perkins, retired editor of *Consumer Reports' Travel Letter*, maintains that Southwest's success lies in not promising more than it can deliver: "They give people what they say they will give them. You go in there with realistic expectations. They never say 'Come fly our luxurious airplanes.'" A client-centric HR department understands its competencies in meeting client's expectations. Then HR staff must meet or exceed those expectations wholeheartedly.

A Service Encounter Must Not Provide
More Than the Client Wants

If customers enter Eat 'n Run, which looks and sounds like a fast-food restaurant, yet see white linen tablecloths, they may feel they are about to experience expensive, leisurely, "fine" dining. People enjoy a fine dining experience, but they want to pick the occasion rather than be surprised when it happens.

Over-delivering on what you can do may be just as unproductive to a client as over-promising on what you cannot. HR staff must be careful not to over-deliver to the point of making managers feel annoyed or uncomfortable. One of the keys here lies in understanding that "time" is typically a manager's most precious commodity. HR employees who understand when they must have the manager's time for face-to-face problem-solving to co-create successful solutions versus solving the problem on their own will foster high credibility and appreciation from line managers.

When does enough become too much? Client-centric HR constantly asks clients what they thought about an experience so that clients do not receive more service than they need or want. As Norman Brinker, the former CEO of Chili's restaurants, said, "Listen to your customers. They'll tell you what to do."

Chapter Takeaways

1. The HR department must take a client-centric approach to delivering HR services by partnering with clients to meet the overall organization's goals.
2. Find the best balance among cost, differentiation, and niche in structuring a client-centric HR department.
3. Manage carefully the "moments of truth" during a service encounter that can make or break how a client views HR staff.

Chapter 3.

Planning to Meet Client Expectations

"Good fortune is what happens when opportunity meets with planning."
—Thomas A. Edison

In the winter of 2007, JetBlue Airways organized meetings of its employees — mechanics, luggage carriers, aircraft cleaners, ramp supervisors, flight attendants, dispatchers, and reservation agents — all across its network to ask them about a fateful day in February when a snowstorm stranded passengers for up to 11 hours on a runway in New York City. By the time the crisis ended, JetBlue had apologized to its passengers, issued millions of dollars in refunds, and its founder, Dave Neeleman, appeared on David Letterman's show to apologize and promote a newly written passenger's Bill of Rights. The positive impact this response had on JetBlue's passenger service reputation was enormous. It had an even greater impact on its employees. The meetings spanned several months to allow team facilitators to put together recommendations on every aspect of the airline's business. Once these recommendations were implemented, JetBlue successfully recaptured its reputation with customers and, just as importantly, with its own employees.

JetBlue learned the simple truth that strategic planning can only take you so far. Unforeseen circumstances, ranging from a natural weather disaster to a competitor's new technology, can disrupt even the most carefully formulated plans. But making plans to meet client expectations — plans underpinned by an inspired vision and focused mission statement — is a critical strength not only for the hallmarks of the service industry but also for client-centric HR departments.

There is an old maxim: "Those who fail to plan, plan to fail." A client-centric HR department becomes truly outstanding by leading managers and their employees where they need to go (even if they do not know it yet) and giving them what they want, when they want it (even if they cannot yet define their wants or needs). In other words, the secret to an HR department becoming client-centric is planning for tomorrow. Planning requires a thoughtful analysis of at least two issues: (1) how the organization's current operating environment — both its strengths and weaknesses — helps and hinders its ability to be successful, and (2) how the organization's future competitive environment — its future opportunities and threats — will require it to change for it to be successful.

This type of planning process means that HR must anticipate what the highly skilled employees needed by the organization in the future will want and will be capable of doing, plan ways to attract them to the organization, and then train them for the jobs of the future. Walt Disney planned an enterprise that he knew would "wow" his customers long before anyone had ever seen a theme park. Disney said, "You don't build it for yourself. You know what the people want and you build it for them." Similarly, telephone customers did not recognize their need for a telephone that can be used anywhere that includes e-mail and texting capabilities until telephone companies made them aware of how useful such a service would be. More recently, people did not know they needed an iPhone or fourth-generation wireless phones until they became available. When they saw how easily they could communicate telephonically or through the Internet, search for information and people, and do other tasks with a tiny instrument they could hold in their hands, they lined up to buy devices that their parents, as kids, had only dreamed about.

The Planning Cycle

An HR planning cycle has three basic steps: (1) an external assessment of the HR department's opportunities and threats, (2) an internal assessment of its strengths and weaknesses, and (3) specific goals and action plans that will enable HR to attain its vision. The external assessment of environmental opportunities and potential threats leads to the formulation of strategic premises about the HR department's future environment. The internal assessment of the HR department's strengths and weaknesses leads to a redefinition or reaffirmation of the department's core competencies and areas for improvement. As can be seen in Figure 3.1, organizational planning follows an ongoing cycle that begins at the big-picture level and ends with goals, budgets, and action plans. (Note: This figure will be referred to throughout the rest of this chapter.)

Figure 3.1

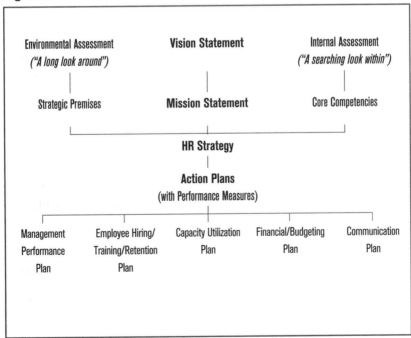

The process shown in Figure 3.1 can help HR make predictions about its future. The plan that results from this process serves as a road map to unite and focus the efforts of HR staff. With a plan in hand, an HR manager can focus staff on the requirements to reach the mission and communicate to those inside and outside HR where the department intends to go, what criteria it will use to allocate resources, and which activities it will pursue or let go.

Service in action: Redefining the Problem

Jeff Cava, now Chief Human Resources Officer, Starwood Hotels & Resorts Worldwide Inc., shared his insights about another large company that was faced with ballooning health care costs growing in excess of 4 to 5 times the consumer price index (CPI). Since the company is self-insured, the increase in costs affected both employee and company bottom lines (the split between costs covered by employee shares of premiums and deductibles covered about 25 percent of total costs and company 75 percent). Increases in costs also acted as a deterrent to many employees from enrolling in the company's health care plans. The bottom line of this problem: Costs were rocketing, affecting the competitiveness of the business

and the pocket books of employees. The response of the business was to increase both premiums and deductibles, and reduce coverage. Employees responded by reducing enrollments and continuing their unhealthy lifestyles.

Asked to solve this problem, the HR department approached the situation by first redefining the problem. Instead of defining it as fixing the current health care plan, it defined it as looking for a "new paradigm" that would accomplish both employee and business goals and as planning a transition strategy. HR defined the problem as behavior management instead of cost management. After a behavioral analysis, the HR staff discovered that users of the plan

Understanding the Environment: External Assessment

The past is not necessarily an accurate indicator for predicting the future. In the early days of the telephone, the ratio of phones to operators was very small. If population trends and the phone-operator ratio had been used to predict the number of telephone operators that would be needed in the distant future, telephone companies would have initiated major recruiting and training programs to

experienced no accountability or responsibility for outcomes associated with the cost of the plan; they lacked perception of the connection between lifestyle behavior and cost of care. In fact, care had always been presented as an entitlement. Consequently, HR created a plan to link behavior with financial and health outcomes. HR staff had the courage to challenge employee perceptions that health care is an entitlement by showing that high satisfaction with health and benefit programs did not correlate with a healthier workforce, nor did it increase employee productivity. By changing the high-cost, low-deductible health insurance strategy with heavy emphasis on incentives and preventive care features, HR saved the business considerable amounts of money.

The results have been very positive, both financially and in terms of real and positive behavior change, financial outcomes (for both employer and employee), and indications of improving trends in overall health. Moreover, the success of the plan has led to increased enrollment rates, health capital accumulation, utilization of preventive care, and dramatically reduced costs for the business and employee. For this innovative response to changes in health care costs, the HR department has been recognized for its unprecedented response to a pressing problem. The strategy proposed has become a dominant strategy for U.S. business.

attract half the people in Canada and the United States to work as telephone operators. Instead, unpredicted but major improvements in technology and work productivity greatly increased the ratio of telephones to operators. The point here is that any forecast based only on the past can be thrown off by unanticipated technological,

---

Service in Action: Stora Enso

When Stora Enso appointed a new CEO, HR Director Gary Parafinczuk immediately asked a consulting company to perform a benchmark analysis that indicated best practice costs for all support functions, including HR, finance, purchasing, and IT. HR's costs were above the benchmarks. Gary's goal for his team was the following: "Develop a plan showing how you will reduce your costs to the benchmark for HR." This assignment was difficult. First, the HR staff had to validate, or in some cases invalidate, the consultant's data, while finding accurate data. Once HR had credible data, HR staff developed a plan and made strategic choices as to how they would operate at the benchmarked cost levels.

Strapped for cash and under pressure to cut Stora Enso's health care costs, Parafinczuk introduced a new paradigm for employees regarding their health care coverage:

In simple terms we could have told our employees that we will keep the current plan and then just keep asking them to pay more each year. Or, we could go to a totally new concept — a "consumer-driven health care plan" — and make it succeed in a way whereby their quality health care continued, and their share of the increased cost would be lower over the long term. We implemented this program with a more than an 80 percent approval rating from the employees after the first year. The program indeed delivered quality health care at a much lower cost than the traditional plan that we had discontinued.

economic, social, environmental, and political changes. As mutual fund salespeople are fond of saying, "Past performance does not guarantee future returns." Rather, imagining and anticipating the effects of changes are keys to planning effectively.

For example, when the automobile first became readily available, some astute people predicted that this new technology would lead to increasing numbers of travelers who would need roadside hotels. Later, others predicted that the legislation that led to deregulation of the airline industry would lead to new airlines, increased competition, lower fares, and more travelers. Walt Disney foresaw the impact of sound on movies, television on entertainment, and the interstate highway system on accessibility to a theme park. In the late 1960s and early 1970s, the Weyerhaeuser HR department foresaw the increasing number of females who would be graduating from business schools with MBAs. It also foresaw the growth of a multicultural workforce. Consequently, it developed workshops for women in management as well as workshops on creating a cultural climate of tolerance and respect for "leading across differences."

Making predictions about the future is necessary for deciding where to put your HR resources, what kind of employees you will need, and what they must know to manage the future organization. Being a little wrong in the forecast is better than not forecasting at all; the decisions about tomorrow must be made today. To come up with the best possible forecast, HR managers can take one of several paths. Although there are many tools for forecasting (see endnotes for suggested readings), we will spotlight only brainstorming and focus groups here.

Brainstorming

Asking a group of people to ponder the future and what it may mean based on what they already know is the nature of brainstorming. Walt Disney said, "We get in there and toss ideas around. And we throw them in and put all the minds together and come up with something." The best ideas often emerge in an open group

Service in Action: Wendy's International Inc.

Dave Thomas, founder of Wendy's, told how his external assessment of business conditions in the late 1960s led to certain premises on which his corporate strategy was based. In planning for his new restaurant concept, he identified five trends he thought offered a market opportunity that he had the competence to meet:

1. *People wanted choices.* They were tired of living in a prepackaged world; they wanted some influence over the products they were buying in the marketplace, and they wanted something new.

2. *People were fed up with poor quality.* He saw a growing interest in foods that are fresh and natural.

3. *People were trying to adjust to a newer, more complicated way of life.* Older people were looking for relief from the many social and political changes, and younger people were looking for changes they could handle. Dave once noted, "In a funny way, the old-fashioned decor and the Tiffany lamps provided a novelty for the young adults and nostalgia for the older generation at the same time."

discussion. Sharing ideas sparks the generation of new ideas. The sum total of those ideas is usually a more accurate forecast than the forecast of any one person. Disney's successful use of "imagineering" in its creative planning department shows that placing creative people in discussion sessions can provoke new ways of looking at things.

Focus groups

Focus groups are another way to pinpoint trends for the future. HR can ask its clients to "focus" on an issue and discuss their thoughts about it with a group discussion leader. Focus groups are most frequently used in assessing the quality of service already rendered, such as line manager interactions with HR. They can

4. *People were on the move.* A smart business had to accommodate this restless mobility.

5. *People were ready for an upscale hamburger place.* He felt that many people had grown up loving hamburgers but were not satisfied with the quality of the food generally available at fast-food outlets.

Thomas wrote the following:

Knowing these five trends allowed Wendy's to focus on the right market. My bet is that if you looked at any successful business, you would find factors very much like these behind that business' success. If you're going to bet your bankroll on a business concept, you had better be able to understand those forces. If you can't describe them, you had better feel them so clearly in your gut that you know you're right.

also be helpful in forecasting what people are apt to like and not like in the future such as a new HR policy, strategy, or process. If your HR department has an innovation in mind, you can quickly form a focus group that is demographically representative of your organization's employees and see how the group reacts to the innovation. For example, different groups of employees could be used to predict the effect of various monetary incentive plans on job performance.

An HR department must assess the uncertain future in terms of potential changes in demographics, technology, governmental regulations, social expectations, economic forces, unexpected disasters, and even potential competitors. Below are some prime examples.

Service in Action: NORPAC

The vision statement at the NORPAC newsprint facility is "The Thinking Person's Mill." Although it is a nonunion plant, it sits in the middle of unionized facilities in a pro-union town, Longview, Washington. A reason why NORPAC has been successful in remaining nonunion is that the HR department constantly works to make certain that the company's vision moves beyond rhetoric to reality. This goal is accomplished through regularly scheduled brainstorming sessions with employees on ways to make NORPAC an ideal employer. It starts with the hiring process, when the expectation is set for new staff that all employees are required to participate in brainstorming sessions to improve newsprint quality, customer service, and anything else that will help NORPAC stay competitive.

Demographics and Education

As more and more government dollars are directed away from education, client-centric HR departments can define themselves as "white knights" to public schools. They can find innovative ways to promote their commitment to the educational and socially responsible values of their present and future employees while helping schools achieve their educational mission. The production of support lesson plans, videos, "edutainment," and electronic media represent prime opportunities for HR departments to provide an invaluable service for public school systems while establishing their organization's brand as socially responsible. Similarly, teachers, who are typically underpaid, may earn supplemental income teaching employees on the job site at the end of the workday.

Net Generation in the Workforce

The divergence between the "haves" and the "have-nots" in the present Information Age is wide among today's school children who are the employees of tomorrow. At the elementary-school level, children of higher-income families who have continuous access to computers and other technology are educationally outstripping those who do not. While basic computer access in schools has helped narrow the gap, those who enter the workforce without the most advanced computer skills will represent a major training and development challenge for organizations that depend on computer-savvy employees. The challenge will be to keep this new group of employees, especially the "have-nots," competitive with the rapidly emerging, highly educated workforce of Asian countries that are already investing heavily in education and training. The workforce is rapidly becoming global. Hence, individuals from many nations are competing for the same jobs. Advances in technology and communication are making employees' location less of an issue to organizations than their skills.

Service in Action: Stora Enso

Gary Parafinczuk had to make a difficult decision to change the retiree health care plan coverage as part of the wholesale changes the HR staff were making to improve its overall personnel cost position. He reports the following:

> We had the richest plan in the industry and we couldn't afford to continue it. While there was no doubt from management that we needed to make a change, *how* we made the change would impact the overall reaction and acceptance of the change by our workforce.

Parafinczuk used an outside consultant to form focus groups of retirees who listened to the company's case for change and gave their reactions to it. While no one liked the idea of changing this valued benefit, the process educated them on the reasons the plan had to change, and the focus groups gave HR valuable feedback on how best to implement it.

The next generation of workers will be very different from today's. As the first generation to have easy access to worldwide communication through the Internet, members of the younger Net Generation will define their interests globally, their "friends" electronically, and their social skills on how they tweet, "update their status," or disseminate information in the blogosphere. Constantly connected to the Internet, they have a global perspective, and as a result they bring a greater diversity of thinking than older members of today's workforce.

Technology

Dramatic changes in technology, especially web-based technology, will continue to have a major influence on both the HR department and the employing organization. Because changes in technology occur so rapidly, their impact is difficult to forecast.

Tara Mauk Arthur, PHR, is the Senior Vice President of Human Resources with Selected Funeral & Life Insurance Company. In addition, she is a member of the Membership Advisory Council (MAC) of the Society for Human Resource Management (SHRM). Arthur has reported that SHRM, with its more than 250,000 members in 150 countries, has been routinely asked by its members to add Facebook and LinkedIn capabilities to help influence legislators and enlighten CEOs on evidence-based HR management practices through these and other social networking sites.

Today, anyone with a laptop, iPhone, BlackBerry, or iPad with Internet access can do thousands of things that previously required a trip out of the house. Take travel for instance: Travelers can now search for the lowest airfare to a destination, make a plane reservation, book a hotel room, and reserve a rental car from wherever they are — transactions that even 10 years ago were time-consuming and required physical trips to a travel agent, plus numerous phone calls. Last century's comic-strip fantasy was Dick Tracy's two-way wrist radio. In this century, smart phones and similar technology have turned this fantasy into a reality. The challenge for HR is to determine how it can use evolving technology to reduce costs in ways that employees will see a positive increase in HR service quality. Many organizations now have online job postings, initial job screening, performance appraisal, succession planning, and real-time training.

E-mail and web-enabled communications are examples of technology already available to HR. Internet-based inquiry systems are convenient for nearly everyone, take less time, and are considerably cheaper for an HR department than hiring HR staff to perform such tasks manually. When a client can access information and answers 24/7/365, the substitution of technology for people typically increases an employee's perception of service quality and value. But using technology to HR's advantage requires a delicate balancing act. In contrast to the above example, most employees and job applicants are annoyed when they call to talk to an HR employee but cannot get through until they punch several phone keys, if then. In those instances, technology decreases perceptions of an HR department's value.

Government Regulations and Social Expectations

Because HR deals directly with managers and their employees, it must confront and respond to an array of government regulations. For example, the Family and Medical Leave Act, which mandates what employers in the U.S. must allow for maternity and paternity leave from the workplace, is among the most demanding and challenging of these. This legislation often leads to an increase in costs for an organization. Similarly, the health care reform legislation enacted in 2010 has created enormous reporting requirements for most organizations.

An HR department may be subjected to the effects of changing social expectations, even when legislation is not in play. Myriad interest groups may seek to influence HR departments. For example, if HR starts offering health and other benefits to same-sex partners, religious groups opposing same-sex relationships may well ask their members to boycott that organization's products or services. Because most organizations depend on maintaining a good relationship with the public, they are vulnerable to attacks by interest groups who disagree with the organization's human resource policies and practices.

As a result, HR leaders must stay abreast of shifting social expectations. Obtaining input from relevant social groups will enhance an HR department's strategic planning process. When planning began for Disney's Animal Kingdom theme park, the organization invited representatives of environmental and animal-rights groups to help in the development process. By working with them, Disney was able to develop a park consonant with their ideals. Similarly, for the HR department, flexible work scheduling is among the most demanded benefits by employees, and setting the proper controls for it are among the most challenging issues for an HR department.

Global Economy

The global economy impacts organizations in many ways. Even the local Italian restaurant depends on factors driven by the global economy when buying the best cheese, wine, and olive oil from Italy. The rise and fall of the Euro against the dollar, as well as production and demand levels, will spur price changes and lead to a rise and fall in profits. On a larger scale, global companies — whose employees may live far beyond their headquarter countries — depend extensively on the HR department to know what adjustments need to be made in both organizational and HR policies to accommodate the differing employee rules, government laws, and economic conditions that will impact their employees. For example, currency fluctuations are a constant, and this issue is always present for HR when dealing with wage rates, expatriate contracts, and other HR issues associated with a global workforce. Premier global companies such as Siemens AG have developed HR processes, procedures, and compensation packages that enable its employees to thrive in an international marketplace. For example, their HR department offers employees on expat assignments the opportunity to learn the language of the country where they will be assigned before moving there. It also trains them on cultural differences and develops a career planning package, so they will know where they will be reassigned upon completion of the assignment.

Competition

The underlying issue here is attracting and retaining the talent the organization will need to be successful in the future it anticipates. To prepare for the future it forecasts, the HR department must develop strategic propositions about what it will need to do to ensure the organization has the workforce necessary to meet its mission and achieve its vision. Will workers be ready, willing, and able to perform the tasks and meet the goals of the future organization? HR must design and gain management acceptance for the employment contract that future employees will want. HR must do all these things if it wants to meet the goal of attracting and retaining talented employees.

Economic and Natural Disasters

When economies melt down or natural disasters happen, HR is the department the organization turns to for solutions to problems such unexpected crises create. While most organizations develop disaster plans for the expected, the unexpected cannot be readily planned. When a banking failure causes payrolls to become problematic or a hurricane destroys the building and many employees' homes, HR takes on the tasks that fix or improve the situation for the organization and its employees. It finds temporary quarters, secures emergency relief and funds, helps identify the missing, and sees that the injured are attended to. In other words, HR is the department that makes disaster recovery happen. Here is where a client-centric HR department truly distinguishes itself by doing what needs to be done efficiently and with compassion.

Whether it is a person stuck in the middle of a political crisis in an unsettled nation that needs protection or even evacuation, or an employee that lost everything in a tsunami, the HR department helps the organization show its human resources how much it cares about them and how vital they are to the organization's success.

Understanding the HR Department: Internal Assessment

On the right side of the planning model in Figure 3.1, opposite "the long look around," is the internal audit, a "searching look within." No HR department can plan with confidence until it confronts its weaknesses and identifies its core competencies. Knowing its competencies enables an HR department to make two principal decisions: what it should do and what it should not do.

When InBev bought Anheuser-Busch, it sold off the SeaWorld division. The acquiring company decided that a theme park was not part of its core competency, namely making beer. Similarly, when the HR department strays from its core competence, it may find itself committing scarce resources to ill-suited activities and not giving the time and attention to the tasks it should. It may wind up pitting its weaknesses against the strengths of other departments, or worse, external suppliers. Many HR departments, for example, have concluded that their core competencies are in areas that impact their organization at the strategic level and have elected to outsource commodity-type functions (for example, payroll) to free up time and energy to concentrate on the areas where it must deliver high-quality service.

Client-centric HR departments must have knowledge in at least two areas: what their clients need to effectively perform their current jobs, and what their clients need to perform those jobs better in the future. An internal assessment tells an HR department where it stands now, what strengths it must develop, and what weaknesses it must eliminate to build core competencies valued by its clients. If the HR department perceives itself to be strong in career counseling and foresees a unionized workforce, the HR staff should set their sights on advising present employees on the downsides as well as the upsides of unionization and job advancement. If HR sees itself as weak in terms of thinking strategically, it needs to acquire skills in strategic planning and refocus its efforts and energies to better serve its clients on strategy and the implementation of strategy, especially on ways of accelerating employees' internalization of the organization's strategy.

An internal audit includes an assessment of all the HR department's internal assets. Those include its reputation, staff and managerial capabilities, financial resources, and other advantages based on, among other things, cost, technology, niche, and brand. The internal audit should also consider the department's weaknesses in those same areas, taking into account the limitations that the overall organization imposes.

HR should plan for what it must do to sustain its core competencies, whether they are hiring committed employees, developing and training leaders, or other strengths. Marriott Hotels, for example, understands that planning according to its core competencies means not getting into businesses it should not be in. Consequently, Marriott sold its airline catering and restaurant divisions that it had operated successfully for 60 years so that it could focus more time and resources on its core competence, namely running Marriott hotels. Thus, the company decided to further capitalize on this core competence by moving into other segments of the lodging market: Marriott Suites; small-sized, medium-priced Courtyard by Marriott; economy-priced Fairfield Inn by Marriott; extended-stay Marriott Residence Inn; and the upscale Ritz-Carlton. Marriott's strategy has been a success. Similarly, HR must evaluate its core competencies and capitalize on those, while shedding functions that are not viewed as offering value to clients.

With a careful assessment of both the external opportunities and threats and internal strengths and weaknesses, the HR department can turn to matching up the current conditions with what it can do and wants to do in the future. This step begins the process of aligning the mission with internal and external assessments of what the department can do to meet its opportunities and of what it must do to meet its future. If an HR manager has a vision of being a strategic partner with line managers, HR must now specify the goal, the mission and a strategy that will in turn specify paths to make that outcome a reality.

Vision and Mission: HR's Path to the Future

The organization has a vision, mission, and strategic plan, and so too should HR. The starting point for HR's vision, mission, and strategic plan is what the overall organization says it wants to be in the future,

Service in Action: Marriott

Marriott also offers an example of how a careful internal assessment found a deficiency in what Marriott had thought was a competency: having sufficiently dedicated and capable employees. An internal audit revealed that the company needed to address certain characteristics of the lower-paid end of its workforce if it wished to employ this group effectively. The problems with this group included lack of education, poor work habits, inability to speak English, culture clashes, financial woes, inadequate child care, and domestic violence. People did not show up for work when they should have; they left early without an explanation. Marriott recognized that although these employees were available for relatively low pay, they were costly, and they were consuming an excessive amount of management's time. The HR department alleviated these problems by training these employees in dealing with issues of work/life balance, offering classes teaching English, and developing a flextime program to help them better manage their family-work conflicts.

what it thinks it should do to become that, and what it plans to do to get there. Just as the overall organization must do these things in the context of its environment, HR must do them in the context of the overall organization. No HR department can know what it needs to do unless it has taken the time to define where it wants to be.

Once an HR department has ascertained its vision, mission, goals and strategy, it should align its core competencies with them. A *vision statement* articulates the HR department's hopes and dreams. A vision statement unites and galvanizes HR staff to attain a common ideal and communicates to HR clients what HR is all about. The vision for Microsoft's HR department is to create an environment where the very best people can do their very best work. Thus, HR collects 360-degree feedback on the company's top 100 managers to ascertain how well they are doing in the eyes of their bosses, peers, and subordinates in turning this vision into a reality.

A *mission statement* articulates the HR department's purpose and the reason why it exists in the organization. The mission statement defines the path to achieving the vision. It defines how the strategic plan will focus the department on the clients HR will serve, what HR will do to serve them, where HR will provide its service, and when. The mission statement allows everyone to clearly see the connection of strategic premises and core competencies to the vision. Thus, the mission statement guides the HR department's overall strategy that in turn drives its decisions as to what HR services will be offered and how service delivery systems will be designed. These decisions lead to action plans that put resources in place to fulfill those plans. Once the planning process is complete, the cycle begins again in a predefined time frame. The planning process cycle never stops because the world in which an HR department operates never stops changing.

In the middle of the model in Figure 3.1 are HR's vision and mission statements. A great deal of time should be spent articulating these concepts because if you do not know what you need to do, it is highly unlikely that you will ever do it.

Defining the Vision Statement

What should the HR department look like in the future, and what significant contributions should it expect to make? The answers to these questions form the basis for a vision. Former Chili's CEO Norman Brinker said, "When it comes right down to it, I do one thing: I have a vision, then I create an atmosphere that involves the people in that vision." Through a vision, the big picture of hopes for the future can be specified. Strategy experts Gary Hamel and C. K. Prahalad call a vision the "quest for industry foresight." An HR department's vision defines what its future could be and works backward to what it must do today to create that future. Hence the purpose of a vision is to galvanize and focus your HR staff. It provides insight that incites people to take action to create a desired future. The vision fosters constructive discontent with the present.

Excellent vision statements are best expressed in one or two sentences. The reverse side of the Extended Stay America card reminds managers of the 2-Minute Rule: "Spend two minutes a day with each employee, taking an interest in that person's life." As noted earlier, NORPAC's vision statement is "The Thinking Person's Mill." Every employee is responsible for thinking about how to increase product quality at the lowest cost.

Defining the Mission Statement

An HR department's mission statement connects to the vision statement by defining who the HR department serves, why HR exists, and what HR should do. It guides HR managers as they allocate resources to specific areas, focuses HR efforts on client-centric activities, and defines for HR staff members how they should treat their clients. Upscale department store chain Nordstrom Inc. offers one of the more famous examples of excellent customer service, as defined by its one-sentence mission statement in its employee handbook: "Use your good judgment in all situations." The simple yet elegant mission of The Ritz-Carlton, winner of a Malcolm Baldrige Quality Award, is the following: "We are Ladies and

Gentlemen serving Ladies and Gentlemen." This mission is printed on a pocket-sized laminated card and is carried by all employees to constantly remind them of what the company believes in, what it expects of its employees, and what service qualities it values. Also printed on that card are the company's credo, its three steps of service, and its twenty basic service standards. They are known collectively as the company's "Gold Standards." In describing the card, former President and Chief Operating Officer Horst Schulze said, "Every employee has the business plan of The Ritz-Carlton in his or her pocket, constantly reinforcing that guest satisfaction is our highest mission." This pocket card has become so famous that many organizations now do the same thing in their efforts to move their vision, mission, and values from a forgotten desk drawer into the minds of employees on a daily basis.

An organization's mission statement often includes its core values. Wal-Mart's founder, Sam Walton, combined mission and values when he said, "[We put] the customer ahead of everything else. ... If you're not serving the customer, or supporting the folks who do, then we don't need you." In summary, a mission statement provides straightforward guidance to HR staff members as to how HR managers expect them to act in their jobs. One HR department stated its mission as: "We put serving our line managers and their employees first, ahead of everything else we do. There is no human resources department without human resources. They are why we are here." How would line managers and managers of other staff functions in your organization react if this mission statement was promulgated by your HR department?

Developing a Service Strategy

Once external and internal assessment factors have been examined and compared to the vision and mission, the HR department is ready to define its service strategy. A client-centric service strategy should result in a set of well-thought-out action plans. Thus, defining a service strategy is critical to HR's effectiveness because it provides a plan for how to make every HR decision — from budgeting to employee programs — in a way that helps the overall organization reach its vision and mission. While predicting the future may make defining and creating an HR service strategy feel as much like art as science, it is still an important blueprint for a client-centric HR department that knows its effectiveness depends on its ability to anticipate and meet its clients' future needs, wants, and expectations.

Chapter 1 discussed the major components of a service organization as service product, service setting, and service delivery system. In this step of the strategic planning process, an HR client-centric service strategy must be translated into specific goals and action steps. If the HR mission is to deliver a service to an upscale, educated workforce, then the service delivery system should be high touch, and the service environment should be congruent with what an upscale workforce expects. On the other hand, if the mission is to deliver a service to an uneducated, low-paid,

Service in Action: Walt Disney Co.

As a strong believer in identifying key drivers, Disney surveys and studies its guests constantly. In one such survey, Walt Disney World Resort guests were asked a variety of questions about their experiences, and how those experiences related to both their intention to return to the parks and their overall satisfaction with the Walt Disney World Resort. Fast food in the parks and the transportation system (other than monorails) received relatively low ratings. However, an analysis of the data revealed only a weak statistical relationship between these low ratings and both intention to return and overall satisfaction with Walt Disney World Resort. On the other hand, ratings of hours of operation, cast member friendliness, cleanliness, and fireworks were strongly related to and largely unskilled workforce, then the service delivery system should be likewise attuned to the needs, wants, and capabilities of these employees. Since most HR departments deliver services to a variety of clients, one-size service will not fit all. Knowing what each client wants and needs from the HR department takes us back to a pertinent lesson from the first chapter: Ask your clients what they want, and observe what they do in order to find out what their real HR needs actually are. Design your strategic goals and actions around client wants, needs, and capabilities. The steps to developing a strategic plan for attaining HR's mission begin here.

Without a plan for providing clients with quality and value, nothing else HR staff members do matters. Although the obvious way an HR department provides value is through its expertise, there are many other ways that HR can bring value to the organization in many other ways. Examples of these value-added "extras" abound in the service industry. The many people who pay extra for personal shoppers in retail stores receive good value for the money they spend in the form of time saved by having

both the intention to return and the client satisfaction measure.

Guided by these survey results, Disney developed a plan to invest its funds in extending park hours, training its cast members, enhancing its cleaning efforts, and expanding the fireworks displays. Although the organization felt competent to improve fast food and the transportation system, it nevertheless allocated resources to improving areas of considerable consequence to customers — the things they said they valued most. In short, the strategic planning process did not just involve managers looking introspectively at organizational core competencies with consultants; it specifically incorporated the wishes and expectations of customers into these decisions.

someone shop for them. J.P. Morgan Chase's HR department pays for meals delivered to the office when an employee works late. The employees save time not having to cook at home or get takeout, so they can spend extra time on the job. An HR department can provide other "extras" such as workshops on retirement, dealing with divorce, caring for aging parents, and ways to make prudent financial investments. Offering such benefits fills significant client needs. As noted earlier, a client-centric HR department measures the perceived value of its services to its clients to demonstrate that they are getting both quality and value from HR.

Another consideration in HR planning is the organization's future staffing needs. An HR department can reinforce its commitment to delivering great service by hiring HR staff who believe in client-centric service, by creating training programs that emphasize commitment to service quality, by allocating resources that empower line managers and their employees to achieve their goals, and by designing reward systems with objective metrics.

Finally, a well-designed HR strategic plan should foster innovation and achievement. Starting in the 1960s, Taco Bell trained its employees so it could operate 90 percent of its company-owned restaurants without a full-time manager. According to Len Berry, "These locations are team-managed by their mostly younger person crews who order inventory, schedule work hours, and recruit and train, among other functions."

From Plans to Action

Action plans represent an organization's decisions on how to best implement its service strategy in specific terms that motivate and guide employees toward accomplishing the vision and implementing the strategic plan with excellence. These plans lay out the specifics of how everyone in the HR department will operate, how results will be measured, and what needs to get done in a specific time period.

The bottom tier of Figure 3.1 indicates the five principal areas in which an HR department should establish action plans: management, staffing, capacity utilization, finance, and communications. Client-centric HR departments look to the overall organization's plans in each of these areas to identify and plan for ways that HR can better assist each manager and department in reaching or exceeding their goals. They also make sure that each area has an appropriate means for measuring the degree to which those plans are achieved. Not only must the HR staff understand the direction in which every client in the organization is supposed to go; HR staff must also know what "getting there" looks like. Measures ensure that the right things are done correctly, that the right goals are attained, and that HR staff members can see how well they themselves are doing as they work toward attaining their goals. Good plans are accompanied by good measures of goal attainment, so everyone knows whether the strategic plan is effective.

No staffing or capacity utilization plan should be set without taking into account the financial/budgeting plan. Similarly, no performance plan should be set without identifying the necessary resources that will allow HR staff to reach their targeted goals. Just as it makes no sense to allocate too many resources to a staffing plan without considering the budget, it also makes no sense to set performance goals without determining what resources an HR department will need to reach those targets.

Although the strategic planning model shown in Figure 3.1 is orderly, the world is not an orderly place. Contingency plans are required to meet changing circumstances.

The need to plan for the probable, and to be nimble enough to react quickly and appropriately if the improbable occurs, suggests another important point: Bring as many different minds to HR's strategic planning process as possible. Increasingly, client-centric HR departments, such as NORPAC's, are including employees with diverse backgrounds in the planning processes. They have learned that good things come from widespread employee participation,

Service in Action: Wal-Mart

A Wal-Mart store in Louisiana had a shoplifting problem, so the HR manager stationed an elderly man at the door to "greet" customers as they entered and left. Potential shoplifters learned that someone would be observing them directly as they left. Even more significantly, honest customers were impressed by his friendly touch. This idea spread to other stores. Today, Wal-Mart has become known in many places for its friendly greeters, as has Holt Renfrew department stores in Canada by following a similar strategy. Was this success the product of strategic planning? The Wal-Mart HR manager responded, "We live by the motto, 'Do it. Fix it. Try it.' If you try something and it works, you keep it. If it doesn't work, you fix it or try something else." The HR manager "tried it." It worked far better than the manager thought it would, so the entire company kept it.

and they understand what makes their clients happy and what does not. To implement an HR strategic plan effectively means that everyone must understand and accept its logic. What better way to gain understanding and to obtain client buy-in than to have clients co-create HR's strategic plan? After all, if clients understand HR's strategic plan and how the plan will guide the organization as a whole, why would they not support it? The best plan in the world is worthless unless those who must make it work truly want to make it work.

When everyone in the HR department is responsible for thinking strategically about the actions to take to fulfill its vision, mission, goals, and strategic plan, the power of individual creativity can be unleashed in very positive ways. The HR planning process should include the people who must make the plan become a reality.

Chapter Takeaways

1. Assess the external environment: What changes might impact HR staff and the organization's employees?

2. Assess the internal organization: What are the HR department's core competencies, and why are they core strengths of the department? What are the weaknesses?

3. Align the anticipated external threats and opportunities, as well as the internal core competencies, with the vision. They all should be simultaneously considered to drive the strategic planning process.

4. Know which HR core competencies will be needed to build for the future.

5. With the vision, mission, and goals in mind, develop a client-centric strategy.

6. Get input from HR clients to define the department's vision, mission, and goals.

Chapter 4.
Creating and Leading a Client-Centric Culture

"Remember we can't change employee behavior without changing ours. We have to have employees who think for themselves. ... We're asking them to see the company's interest as their own and to voluntarily take responsibility."
— Isadore Sharp, founder and CEO, Four Seasons Hotels and Resorts

When you fly on Southwest Airlines, shop at Nordstrom, or stay at a Four Seasons hotel, you can sense something special about those organizations and the people who work there. People invariably describe their experience as better than they had expected. What is even more enlightening is how the employees tell you how their respective organizations differ from other companies. For example, both Four Seasons and Nordstrom employees talk about their organization's commitment to customer service; Southwest Airlines employees talk about their commitment to providing a unique and pleasurable flying experience. Not only do employees talk about the values of their respective companies, but they believe in them, and they live them at these benchmark companies. These employees enthusiastically show their commitment to their organization's values daily in a thousand different ways.

Leadership plays a crucial role in creating and sustaining the service culture of an organization. Herb Kelleher of Southwest Airlines and Isadore Sharp of Four Seasons Hotels and Resorts spent the personal time and energy necessary to create and sustain their organization's culture to define the values for which their respective organizations are now famous. These leaders communicated their commitment to client-centric service through their words and deeds, clearly and consistently, to those inside and outside their respective organizations.

Can others, even those who are not presidents or founders of an organization, similarly influence an organization's culture? The answer is yes. Most employees try to behave as their supervisors do, and supervisors in turn are influenced by the behavior of their managers. The role models for most employees are an organization's senior-level managers, especially the organization's leader. A leader is the role model for the entire organization and hence the person who ultimately defines and inculcates an organization's cultural values. As Sharpe noted in the quote at the beginning of this chapter, "Remember, we can't change employee behavior without changing ours." As an HR manager, you have the power to instill a client-centric culture in your department.

Culture = Reputation

The HR culture, like a person's character, drives its reputation. An HR department that provides client-centric service in a truly respectful and helpful way to managers and their employees can be assured an excellent reputation throughout the organization. A culture is nothing more than the values, beliefs, and norms of an HR department. Leaders of client-centric HR staff consistently reaffirm and support client-centric values. Consequently, HR staff quickly learn that providing excellent service to clients is what "they must do."

Creating and maintaining a client-centric culture requires consistency and effort. An HR manager must devote time to constantly remind staff of client-centric values and reinforce those values at every opportunity by word and deed. Walt Disney admonished, "Never let your personnel get sloppy. Never let them be unfriendly." If you see HR staff doing something inconsistent with a client-centric culture and you ignore it, as an HR leader you send the message to your staff that this behavior is a legitimate option. After several instances of an HR manager saying one thing, but neither rewarding the proper action nor punishing the improper action, everyone throughout the organization will know that HR leadership's real level of commitment to its client-centric values is low. On the other hand, when you as an HR manager publicly and vociferously celebrate behaviors that are consistent with client-centric values, you send a strong signal that those client-centric values go far beyond just words. Both are essential, but as everyone knows, actions speak louder than words.

Disney provides an outstanding example of an organization that has worked hard to define and sustain a strong culture. Culture is so valued by Disney that it is explicitly defined in the employee handbook. In addition to the words in a book, the Disney managers stress culture verbally to cast members. According to *Inside the Mouse* by Jane Kuenz, employees

> "are frequently people who have migrated to Orlando specifically to work at Disney, often with exceedingly high, perhaps naive, expectations about the park. While these expectations are sometimes vague notions that Disney must be "the epitome of the fun place to work," at other times they reflect a high level of personal investment with the park and with its power to raise the innocuous or mundane lives of average people into the fantastical and magical existence of the Disney cast member."

In short, culture attracts employees to organizations where they find others with like-minded values. Many people believe so strongly in Disney's ability to create a magical experience for its guests that they want to become a part of that magic. Thus, Disney expects their managers to be responsible for ensuring service excellence no matter where they work in the resort and to observe and coach every employee to meet service standards.

Culture as Competitive Advantage

Culture can be a competitive advantage both in competing for customers and for employees. Southwest Airlines' strong client-centric culture offers it a competitive advantage in both attracting the type of employee Southwest desires and in attracting customers who expect Southwest's type of service. The company's culture can be seen by how Southwest describes it:

> "The 'Southwest Spirit' is the twinkle in your eye, the skip in your step; it is letting that childlike spirit escape and be heard. To know what really makes Southwest Spirit, you have to look beyond the machines and things because running a fun and productive airline defies science; it is an art that comes from working hard with feeling."

People who find this definition to be corny are unlikely to apply for or be hired by Southwest Airlines.

Working in a culture where the HR staff has the "spirit" to look beyond machines to the art of providing service to clients is different from working in a traditional HR department. More importantly, HR clients who encounter a "client-spirited" HR culture similar to Southwest's usually find it both uniquely tuned to their needs and, well, fun. By creating a "spirited" culture where HR staff visibly display client-centric values, the HR department stands to win the enduring support of other managers and their employees across the organization.

Management by Culture

Isadore Sharp, the founder and CEO of Four Seasons, tells his managers that the stronger the culture, the less necessary it is to rely on bureaucratic management controls — policies, procedures, and managerial directives. A strong culture minimizes reliance on control mechanisms. The delivery of HR's client-centric service must be underpinned by strong HR management cultural values, ensuring that well-trained and empowered HR staff members provide the right services for their clients, giving them what they need when they need it and where they need it. Clients are not passive. They frequently do whatever they think is the quickest way to solve their problems and to attain their goals, often with little or no thought to HR policies or procedures. When HR creates a strong client-centric culture the staff engage clients in ways consistent with that culture. The culture itself will guide those staff to do the right things right even when the HR manager is not nearby. The experience other managers have with an HR department is subject to incredible variation; as many different things can happen as there are different types of clients. Since defining and preparing for all the possibilities is impossible, an HR manager must rely on staff to understand what should be done and then do that for the client the right way every time. The more uncertain the situation or task, the more an HR manager must rely on HR staff member's understanding of and commitment to client-centric values, rather than on formal policies and established procedures, to guide their behavior. When HR staff members do not know what to do, they are likely either to do nothing or to guess and hope for the best. In a client-centric HR department, culture cues the staff to do the right things the right way.

Consider a professional chef. While much of any culinary program is devoted to teaching the principles of proper food preparation, training also instills a passion for consistent excellence in what is prepared. Regardless of program or type of culinary training, this central value is clear: The chef's passion must be constant and consistent to provide flawless production of a fine dining experience for every customer, every time. Indeed, some casual-dining chains have even sent their cooks to culinary courses not so much to learn how to cook, since the chain's recipes are standardized, but to learn respect for the culinary (read: cultural) value of consistently creating high-quality food products. That way the customer at a Chili's or Olive Garden, like the customer at a five-star Parisian restaurant, will have a consistently well-prepared meal.

Culture, Inside HR and Out

A strong HR culture enables HR staff members to deal with two core issues: (1) how to relate to clients and (2) how to relate to people inside their department — that is, other staff.

When an HR department has an "us versus them" mindset, staff members will be unreceptive to ideas from their clients, secretive about what their department is doing, and protective of its "proprietary knowledge." On the other hand, a client-centric HR culture constantly encourages the growth and development of staff as they interact with other departments in the organization, benchmark against best-practice HR departments wherever they can be found, and listen to and consider ideas and innovations developed outside the HR department. Not surprisingly, client-centric HR departments adapt quickly to changes in clients' expectations and respond effectively to their needs.

Soosan Latham, a former Vice President of Human Resources at J.P. Morgan, describes how the HR department behaved as a partner to the bank's business units. She realized that the only way to be an effective partner with these units was for HR to be open to clients' needs, wants, and expectations. For example, upon taking the leadership role in HR, Latham went directly to the investment banking unit and asked the manager and employees what they needed from HR in order to be effective. She asked specifically about recruitment and retention issues as well as training and development needs. The knowledge she gained from this proactive strategy increased HR response time in helping investment banking solve its HR challenges. Latham acted on the simple truth that for the HR department to be effective, it must collaborate with the organization's business units to successfully co-produce solutions to their HR challenges.

In many ways, big and small, the HR culture dictates how staff interact with each other to accomplish the department's mission. Culture-based assumptions guide HR staff members in making decisions about that which they control, including their functional areas, interpersonal relationships, and attitudes toward clients. For example, at J.P. Morgan Chase, Soosan Latham instilled in her staff the importance of reinforcing client-initiated HR processes. When a feedback process developed by a business manager proved successful, HR staff subsequently championed its use to other business managers without any attempt to claim ownership.

Creating a Culture of Service

As an HR manager, how do you create and sustain a client-centric culture? How do you blend a service-oriented culture in HR into the culture of the overall organization? Furthermore, how best should you communicate the culture to your staff? Everyone has been in an organization that feels warm, friendly, and helpful — perhaps for reasons that cannot be easily articulated. Similarly, everyone has been in an organization that feels cold, aloof, uncaring, and impersonal. How you create and sustain a client centered culture is an HR manager's challenge.

As service management writer Len Berry said,
"Sustained performance of quality service depends on organizational values that truly guide and inspire employees. And how does an organization get such values? It gets them from its leaders who view the infusion and cultivation of values within the organization as a primary responsibility."

Service in Action: Marriott

Bill Marriott Jr. provides a good example of how a leader can help sustain an organization's culture. He constantly teaches, preaches, and reinforces Marriott's cultural values of customer service. Believing in staying visible, he flies more than 200,000 miles every year to visit his many operations and to carry the Marriott message visibly and personally to as many people as he can. He is famous for dropping in at a hotel and chatting with everyone he sees. He has been known to get up early in the morning and wander into the Marriott kitchens to make sure the pancakes are being cooked properly. His intense commitment to personal contact with each and every Marriott employee and his visible interest in the details of operations have become so well known throughout the Marriott organization that even the possibility of his unannounced presence on any Marriott property serves as a reminder of the Marriott commitment to service quality.

If an HR department's client-centric culture is strong, that culture becomes a core competency. As would be true for other core competencies, an HR staff member who seeks to do something incompatible with HR's culture is likely to fail. The HR department that is accustomed to providing a high-quality, client-centric experience will resist — likely with great success — anyone trying to implement a cost-saving move that somehow jeopardizes that service experience. The basic principle underlying a client-centric culture is straightforward: If an HR department is committed to a strategy of service excellence, an HR manager must constantly teach and support a client-centric culture. Otherwise, that culture will not flourish. An HR department's culture is a way of thinking and acting that is fomented by the HR manager and learned and shared by the HR staff. In other words, culture is "the way we do things here."

The Elements of Culture

Client-centric HR departments, knowing that rules and procedures cannot cover everything, spend considerable time defining and teaching the culture to staff so that they know how to act appropriately in their interactions with clients and with one another. Because of their client-centric approach, staff members understand from the start what all the departments in the organization do, what their values are, and how HR can help them solve their problems as a business partner. As noted above, J.P. Morgan Chase's HR department values client-driven initiatives. To plant the seeds for these initiatives, one or more HR staff were assigned to each business unit. This strategy enabled HR to act as a business partner in identifying leadership skills required at different management levels (such as managing director, vice president, associate, or analyst), as well as in understanding training objectives and job performance criteria. Following this approach enabled HR to fill in the inevitable gaps between what can be predicted or planned and what actually happens when clients interact with the HR department.

The core elements of a culture are the following: beliefs, values, norms, and laws.

Beliefs

Beliefs are the ideological core of HR's culture. A belief helps HR staff understand how the HR department should serve its clients in attaining their goals. If HR staff members know that HR rewards those who are client-centric and punishes those who are not, the importance of providing good client service becomes a cultural belief. A client-centric HR manager takes an active role in defining the beliefs that make HR a client-centric department.

Values

Values define for HR staff the behaviors considered to be right or wrong, preferred or not preferred, desirable or undesirable. When an HR manager sends a clear signal to all HR staff that providing good service to clients is a core value, HR staff members are highly likely to behave in ways that create a positive HR experience for their clients.

Norms

Norms are the expectations that an HR department has of its employees in terms of how they should behave, how they should dress and appear, and what they should or should not say to others. A client-centric HR department would have norms, for example, of greeting a client with respect and showing genuine interest.

Norms are defined and shaped not only by peers and the HR leader but also by clients. At the Weyerhaeuser Company, HR staff members are expected to be on the shop floor. When HR employees fail to appear, they are the butt of jokes and snide remarks by the hourly employees when they finally reappear ("Oh, look who now has found time for us."). A norm at J.P. Morgan Chase is never to criticize a client in front of the client's staff.

Laws

The laws of an HR department are its rules, policies, and regulations. They include norms that are so critical they need to be written down, so everyone in the department not only knows exactly what they are, but also know the specific consequences of violating them. The HR department is often thought of as the organization's police officer, ensuring that all employment laws, organizational procedures, and union contract provisions are followed consistently by managers across the organization — many of whom are sufficiently unfamiliar with the organizational repercussions of not following these laws to see HR only as an intrusive cop instead of as a helpful partner. The challenge for a client-centric HR department is for its staff to be seen simultaneously as "lawyers" who help keep clients out of legal difficulties, advisors who share their expertise, and business partners who help clients attain their respective goals.

Communicating the Culture

Client-centric HR departments manage their culture in a holistic way. They reinforce clearly and consistently the values they expect the staff to have in mind when they are working with clients. They do this by communicating HR's culture in myriad ways, including training HR staff on the department's beliefs, values, and norms; developing the department's own rules; demonstrating HR's beliefs, values, and norms through the telling of service stories, legends, and heroes; and providing rewards for culturally desired behaviors.

Employee Training

Since everyone brings to a new job the cultural assumptions from past experiences, client-centric HR managers start teaching HR's values to employees from day one. Often, they are responsible for doing the same for the entire organization.

The "Traditions" training program at Disney is a good illustration. On their first day of employment, employees go to a classroom at "Disney University" where they learn not only about their role in creating the Disney "magic" but also about how their role fits into the traditions, history, and core beliefs of the Disney organization. This experience gives employees a common cultural background and also communicates the significance and meaning of their role in the Disney culture. No matter what function they may perform later, the glue that binds cast members together is the belief that they are all participating in, and contributing to, the primary values that drive the Disney culture. Employees learn four primary values in order of their importance to Disney: safety, courtesy, show, and efficiency. When employees encounter unfamiliar situations in which they have to decide the right thing to do, these four values guide every employee to contribute to Disney's worldwide reputation for service.

J.P. Morgan Chase uses a similar idea based on its reputation as being among the nation's best employers. New recruits come to the company already excited about being part of this famous organization. At its three-day orientation program, all new employees are given not only an overview of the culture and values on which the company was founded, but also a 700-page book about the history and culture of this venerable financial industry powerhouse.

Service in Action: Southwest Airlines

Truly outstanding client-centric HR managers engage their staff in teaching each other the culture. Herb Kelleher, former CEO of Southwest Airlines, knew the importance to the company of sharing the culture to reinforce it, and even created a Culture Committee whose responsibility was to perpetuate the Southwest Airlines "spirit."

The Culture Committee was created to pull together people who exemplify Southwest's culture. Most of the original committee had worked 10 or so years at Southwest and embraced Southwest's maverick, caring, irreverent way of doing things. They were great at their individual jobs and were handpicked for their creativity, expertise, energy, enthusiasm, and most importantly, the Southwest "spirit." For the two years they serve on the committee as members, they engage in leadership activities that enhance the company's unique and highly valued culture. Committee members have been known to visit stations with equipment and paint in hand to remodel a break room. Others have gone to one of Southwest's maintenance facilities to serve pizza and ice cream to maintenance employees. Still others simply show up periodically at various field locations to lend a helping hand. Their labor is really a labor of love. Their payoffs are the relationships they build with other workers, the knowledge that they have sparked worthwhile and fun endeavors, and the satisfaction of having been a vital part of keeping the Southwest "spirit" alive.

Stories, Legends, and Heroes

Stories, legends, and heroes provide an HR manager with another way of transmitting cultural beliefs, values, and norms. They communicate the right and wrong way to do things. American Express uses stories about its employees to teach its culture. It calls those employees who have provided exceptional service to customers "Great Performers." Stories are told about two customer-service employees in Florida who sent money to a woman in an overseas war zone and helped her board a ship out of the dangerous country; travel agents in Columbus, Georgia, who paid a French tourist's bail, so he could get out of jail; an employee who drove through a blizzard to take food and blankets to stranded travelers at Kennedy Airport; and an employee who got up in the middle of the night

Service in Action: The Olive Garden

The Olive Garden restaurant uses stories to teach employees the cultural value of the service it seeks to offer its customers. In its early days when it was trying to teach new employees its corporate culture of customer service, an opening manager would often tell a story about a customer named Larry. It seems that Larry came to an Olive Garden and found the armchairs uncomfortable for his significantly above-average weight. He wrote the company president a letter praising the food yet complaining about the chairs. In response, the Olive Garden ordered and placed in every restaurant two "Larry Chairs" that have no arms. These chairs were to be discretely substituted for normal chairs whenever a person of extra girth came into the restaurant. Needless to say, telling the Larry Chair story at a store opening revealed a great deal about the company's service values. It sent a strong message to new employees about how far they should go to respond to and meet a customer's needs.

to take an American Express card to a customer stuck at Boston's Logan Airport. American Express distributes its Great Performers booklets to all employees worldwide.

Disney uses a host of stories to reinforce its culture. One is about the busy corporate executive from a different company who made time to work at the Magic Kingdom for a few days every month, and another about an heiress who flew in from her own private island to ladle punch at Aunt Polly's landing. While the stories may not always be accurate, they represent a central cultural belief by employees that, according to *Inside the Mouse,* "Walt Disney World is the place where truck drivers' daughters work alongside corporate executives in their common mission of producing magic." In other words, the culture of creating the Disney customer experience is so positively valued that it draws in employees and volunteers, regardless of their social status or position.

Many stories are reported about Walt Disney himself, especially those showing his attention to detail and service excellence. When he died in 1966, he left behind a series of films in which he conducted staff meetings before an empty conference room with the intention, and the result, that they be shown monthly to his senior staff after his death. As one observer reported, he held conferences into the 1970s in which he would make statements such as, "Bob, this is October, 1976. You remember we were going to do this or that. Are you sure it's underway now?" Such attention to detail and commitment to service quality left an enduring legacy. Indeed, for years after Disney's death, managers reportedly made many decisions by first trying to determine "what Walt would have done" or "what Walt would have wanted."

Every HR department can find or invent stories, legends, or heroes that illustrate a cultural value or belief in a memorable way. An HR department needs to do so because people remember richly detailed and emotion-evoking stories long after the PowerPoint presentations with bulleted teaching points have faded from memory.

Connecting with a story of how an HR hero acted is much easier than internalizing a lecture on "client responsiveness" in a formal training class. Not only are stories memorable, but the tales are typically embellished in the retelling, and given powerful emotional punch — thereby bringing a client-centric culture to life. Tales of "ol' Pat" and what wondrous things that individual did while serving clients teach desired responses to client concerns, while simultaneously reaffirming an HR department's values. Every client-centric HR department should capture and preserve the stories and tales of its staff who do amazing things — creating magical moments — to touch line managers and their employees. Doing so yields a wonderful array of inspiring stories for all HR staff and sends a strong message about an HR department's culture.

Subcultures
The more people there are who work in a large organization, the harder it is for them to stay in communication with one another. Consequently, the likelihood is high that subcultures will form. Subcultures can be supportive or destructive, and consistent with or contrary to the HR department culture — not to mention the organization's overarching culture. Since culture is made up of interactions, small groups of people who work closely together may well create a subculture of their own, especially if they do not interact a great deal with other HR units (for example, payroll). HR departments that depend on part-time employees or outsourcing are especially susceptible to the formation of subcultures. These employees may spend too few hours in Human Resources to absorb its culture.

The overall culture of the HR department must be strong enough to override subcultures on issues imperative to the department's client-centric effectiveness. While some cultural variation may be tolerated, the client-centric culture must be defined and reinforced by the HR manager in ways sufficiently clear for both clients and the HR staff to understand the client-centric values of the department. This approach does not mean rigidity in thinking or dogmatic beliefs, but it does mean that the core cultural value of client centricity is accepted and practiced by all HR staff, regardless of area or subgroup.

At J.P. Morgan Chase, while the HR staff was committed to the culture of Human Resources, staff members also adapted to the values of the client they served. Hence, the culture of the HR team supporting the traders was different from the culture of the team serving the investment bankers or the technology groups. In this example, the HR manager, Soosan Latham, viewed her primary role as ensuring that such subcultures supported Human Resources' global commitment to delivering quality service. Latham's outlook showed a client-centric focus at its best because HR staff recognized and responded effectively to the different wants, needs, and expectations of these diverse clients.

Setting the Example

Southwest Airlines is famous for its hands-on commitment to service. Co-founder and first chief executive Herb Kelleher literally walked the talk through airports, airplanes, and service areas to show employees his concern for the quality of each customer's experience. He set an example for the entire company. Even today, this tradition lives on as all Southwest managers are expected to spend time in customer-contact areas, observing as well as working in customer-service jobs. These actions send a strong message to employees that everyone is responsible for maintaining the high quality of the Southwest experience. This same modeling behavior can be seen on the part of Marriott's hotel managers who visibly and consistently stop to pick up scraps of paper and debris on the floor as they walk through their properties. Employees see and consequently emulate this care and attention to detail.

Service in Action: Rosen Hotels & Resorts

Harris Rosen, a leading hotelier in Orlando, has earned a reputation among his employees and fellow hoteliers alike as a "can-do manager." His story began when he bought a bankrupt hotel with very little money and a whole lot of courage. When he was seen mowing his own property's lawn, the legend was born that here was a guy who would do what it took to get the work accomplished. He reinforced this message with his working attire: typically blue jeans and a polo shirt. His employees learned, by reputation and by deed, that this owner was ready to work at any job that needed doing.

Rosen had a big sign on the interstate highway advertising different room rates for each night, and because he was willing to bend with the market winds, he earned a further reputation as a relentless competitor. His strategy was to fill his rooms at rates that would allow him to capture his variable costs plus whatever else the market would bear. His flexibility in room rates and his nightly phone calls to his front-desk manager, asking about the percentage of rooms sold rather than the revenue, sent a powerful message to his organization that the goal was to fill the rooms every night. Through his own actions, dress, and management style, Rosen has been extraordinarily effective in teaching his employees, at all organizational levels, the cultural values and norms that he wants for his organization.

As Rosen showed, it all comes back to leadership. A client-centered HR manager must stay close to both the staff and their clients. Only by walking around can an HR manager judge the quality of the client experience, confirm that the concerns of managers and their employees are being met, and affirm that everyone in HR is focused on the client. As former Chili's Bar and

Grill Chairman Norman Brinker put it, "There's no substitute for spending time with people in their own environment. You not only meet everybody personally, you are able to see and hear for yourself what's going on." The best restaurant managers at Chili's meet as many customers and make as many table visits as possible to talk to them; Marriott's hotel managers wander the lobbies to observe the reactions of customers to its service; and Nordstrom's retail-store managers monitor the looks on customers' faces to make sure the shopping experience is going well. All these strategies are based on the simple truth that the reason for an organization's existence, and the basis for its success, is the customer.

As most HR managers know, the pressures of day-to-day

Service in Action: SAS Group

Upon taking over the ailing Scandinavian Airlines System in 1980, Jan Carlzon recognized the deficiencies in the airline's strategy and its employees' lack of understanding of the airline's mission. He launched a service-quality training program for all 20,000 employees that eventually cost several million dollars at a time when SAS was losing $17 million a year. Because it involved training every employee who worked for the airline, this concept became known as "wall to wall training," given that it was geared toward changing the entire company's culture.

Changing employee attitudes was one of the most significant results of the SAS turnaround strategy. By stating that the company would turn a profit by becoming a service-oriented airline, SAS ignited radical change in its culture. Traditionally, executives dealt with investments, management, and administration. Service was of secondary importance — the province of employees located way out on the periphery of the company. Now the entire company — from the executive suite to the most remote check-in terminal — would be refocused on service.

administrative responsibilities can easily lead to a loss of focus on clients, so they build client contact time into their schedules. Jose Berrios, former Vice President of Human Resources for Gannett Company Inc., a news and information company that publishes *USA Today,*, and chair of SHRM's Board of Directors, tells of his commitment to taking the time to practice MBWA (managing by walking around) as a way to stay proactive and in the loop of what was going on across the organization. By walking around, he heard firsthand what both line managers and their employees were saying about issues that concerned HR. He currently does likewise with SHRM's staff even though doing so requires him to fly regularly from his home in San Antonio to SHRM's headquarters in Alexandria, Virginia.

Carlzon noted the following:

Beyond the attention to service, we were also able to stir new energy simply by ensuring that everyone connected with SAS — from board members to reservation clerks — knew about and understood our overall vision. As soon as we received approval from the board, we distributed a little red book entitled "Let's Get in There and Fight" to every one of our 20,000 employees. The book gave the staff, in very concise terms, the same information about the company's vision and goal that the board and top management already had. We wanted everyone in the company to understand the goal; we couldn't risk our message becoming distorted as it worked its way through the company.

This was the first time a major corporation used a 100 percent training process to help create a cultural change in an organization. Every employee — from shop workers to top managers — went through a two-day workshop on "The New SAS."

Changing the Culture

It is admittedly difficult to change a culture that is not oriented toward service. When Jan Carlzon took over Scandinavian Airlines System (SAS), he was confronted with tough labor unions, disheartened management, a stagnant market, and an obsolete corporate strategy. He knew that the only chance for the airline's survival was to change SAS into a customer-focused organization.

Carlzon had learned about the power of getting employees involved directly in the change process during his earlier experience at Linjeflyg, the Swedish domestic airline that was later absorbed by SAS Group. His first official act after being appointed president of that airline was to call all the staff together in one airline hangar. He climbed a 15-foot ladder and told them the following:

> "This company is not doing well. It's losing money and suffering from many problems. As the new president, I don't know a thing about Linjeflyg. I can't save this company alone. The only chance for Linjeflyg to survive is if you help me — assume responsibility yourselves, share your ideas and experiences so we have more to work with. I have ideas of my own, and we'll probably be able to use them. But most important, you are the ones who must help me, not the other way around."

People left the meeting with a new spirit of enthusiasm and commitment.

Regardless of whether an HR department's culture needs to be updated to accommodate new circumstances and realities, or needs to be recreated altogether, an HR manager must use all available communication tools to bring about and maintain a desired change. As noted at the beginning of this chapter, an essential job of an HR manager is to frame the HR department's culture's beliefs, define its values, reinforce the appropriate norms of behavior, recognize and tell stories about those who personify what the culture should mean, and find every possible occasion to celebrate when HR staff members make good things happen for their clients. If achieving service excellence is imperative to you, then you, the HR manager, must lead your department, conveying clearly and without equivocation that client-centric service is the goal. HR staff will soon believe and behave accordingly with that culture.

A Final Caution

An organization's culture can be a problem. Sometimes it may be so strong that it is unable to change when new developments in the business or the environment require it to do so. SHRM's Board chair-elect, Bette Francis, Vice President/Director of Human Resources, Wilmington Trust Wealth Advisory Services, offers an illustration from her experience in the following textbox.

Service in Action: Changing the culture

A midsized manufacturing organization was led by its president and founder. His philosophy, in combination with the force of his personality, led to the creation of a strong culture oriented toward his beliefs and values. In spite of his paternalism and old-school practices, the employees were given freedom to be creative. Employees could even wear shorts and flip-flops to work. If you were hired into accounting but wanted to help out in purchasing, that was fine too. Hands-on, self-motivated, and self-taught employees thrived in this environment. The organization structure was extremely flat so that everyone was only one layer away from the president/founder. Although pay rates were in the 50th percentile, white collar turnover was low, and sales turnover was zero because sales/customer service was extraordinary. The company ran lean so that it could survive thin margins and economic downturns. The strength of the company, with a clear dominant position in market share, was an incredibly loyal customer base. The customer was king; distributor

continued on next page

Service in Action: Changing the culture

continued from previous page

networks were protected; promises were kept. So solid was the customer base that when a Fortune 500 company entered this niche market with lots of money and manufacturing expertise, it could not make any headway and quit the market after five years of trying to penetrate it.

When the president/founder retired, he left the business on "autopilot." The culture was ingrained. Without a formal leader, problems were solved by an informal network of management peers. The company experienced no loss of sales or reputation during this period, and operations went smoothly. However, because the culture was so strong, the organization lacked an openness to change: it saw no growth from new products or markets, no new sourcing of product, and no other initiatives to adapt to changes in the market and the environment. After five years of operating in this fashion, a new board of directors was assembled to bring in new people with new ideas. This decision represented a 180-degree change that created culture shock for the managers used to the old culture and for the new managers who did not know how to operate in this lean culture. As a result there was a voluntary and involuntary exodus of the "old" managers who felt disenfranchised or who were deemed unable to adapt to the new cultural values and beliefs. The problem was that the incoming managers did not understand the power of a strong existing culture to resist change. In less than five years, hastened by poor economic conditions, the company entered decline and saw the erosion of its solid customer base.

The moral of this story is that a strong culture can be an impediment when the conditions in which that culture was created change. If the culture is not open to change, the organization may die.

Chapter Takeaways

1. HR managers must explicitly and consistently define a client-centric culture by what they say and do.

2. A strong client-centric culture provides staff guidance in uncertain situations where HR policies or procedures do not exist. It fills in the gaps for HR staff between what they have been taught and what they must do to be client-centric.

3. Subcultures invariably form in large organizations. A strong client-centric HR culture increases the likelihood of keeping subcultures consistent with the overall client-centric values.

4. Find heroes, tell stories, and repeat legends to reinforce client-centric values.

5. Creating a true client-centric culture is the responsibility of the HR manager. The importance of leadership in the HR department cannot be overstated.

Chapter 5.
Client-Centric Staffing & Training

"If someone isn't smiling during the interview, what in the world would make you think they will be smiling when faced with a line of customers all in a hurry for service, service, service?"
— T. Scott Gross, author, *Positively Outrageous Service*

A bellhop at a Sheraton Hotel was confronted with an unusual problem. A departing customer had locked his car keys in his trunk while checking out. The car was parked in the middle of the driveway that handled all the arriving and departing traffic and, if not immediately moved, would bring the entire check-in/check-out process to a halt. The bellhop called for a floor jack that he had had the foresight to store away nearby, jacked up the car, and rolled it from the middle of the driveway to the curb. Before the customer became stressed, the bellhop called for a locksmith and told the customer when the locksmith was expected to arrive, promising to keep the customer informed as events unfolded. The traffic problem was solved, the keys-in-the-trunk issue was promptly addressed, and the customer was spared the embarrassment of being the cause of everyone else's delay.

A family was visiting the Walt Disney World Resort's Magic Kingdom. They had come to Orlando from their home in the Midwest and had carefully planned to make this trip truly memorable. One day, toward the end of their visit, they were in the Haunted Mansion attraction, when their little boy lost his Mickey ears during the ride. At the exit, the father asked the ride operator to please look through the cars to see if the ears were there. Those ears were not just a hat to this little boy; they had become his most prized possession, purchased on the first day of the visit and worn faithfully everywhere ever since. The ears were nowhere to be found, and the operator watched sadly as hope died in the little boy's face.

Recognizing that this family's trip to Orlando was about to turn from a "wow" to an "ow," the operator seized the moment and saved the day. She went across the walkway to a souvenir stand, took two Mickey hats, put one on the dad's head and the other, triumphantly, on the little boy's. Not surprisingly, management received a letter of thanks from the parents a few weeks later. This simple act, by an employee committed to service, put smiles back on the entire family's faces. She made this a truly memorable trip for this child and his parents.

Where can an HR department find people who are client-centric? Does the service industry know something that your HR department has yet to discover? Service organizations such as the Four Seasons, Nordstrom, and The Ritz-Carlton know how to hire people who can genuinely deliver client-centric service. In addition, they know how to train them to deliver the service experience their clients want, need — and appreciate.

How often does your HR staff show they are as committed to client-centric service as the Sheraton bellhop or the Disney ride operator? How often do they go "off script" to do something that is so memorable that a client takes the time to thank you, write a letter, or send an e-mail of appreciation? Hiring employees who will provide such service is not easy, but it is by no means impossible. What is more, teaching HR staff how to deliver client-centric service is possible.

Building a Service-Centric HR Team

Author T. Scott Gross devotes a considerable part of his book,

Positively Outrageous Service, to the significance of hiring people who create unique, meaningful memories of service. Spontaneous, extra-role behavior often determines the margin of difference between an "as expected" client experience and one that is truly "outstanding." Whether it is the waiter who bursts into unexpected song during a restaurant meal, the Avis bus driver who delivers a comedic monologue during the ride to an off-airport rental location, or the HR employee who effectively coaches a manager on how to engage in a difficult conversation with the union executive committee, the point here is the same.

HR staff who are recruited, hired, and then trained to provide excellent service for clients add value in at least three ways. First, they make the HR experience memorable in a positive way, which in turn increases the likelihood that line managers will keep HR involved and informed as partners in the business. Second, HR staff who interact with clients in this way create a competitive advantage for the HR department. No outsourced supplier of HR services can design into its HR service experience the same feeling of a customized connection with clients that well-selected, properly trained, internal HR professionals can provide. Third, the opportunity to provide outstanding HR service for the client is, for an HR staff member, a terrific opportunity to "shine." By encouraging staff to take every opportunity to be seen as the HR "can do" person with creative problem-solving skills and the ability to make emotional connections with clients, an HR manager conveys to the staff how much their skills are valued and that they are trusted to do the "right things." For people who sought a job in HR for the opportunity to demonstrate their creativity and originality, serving clients is a meaningful and even fun part of their job.

Research shows that customers generally draw upon five criteria to judge the overall quality of the service they receive. Of these five, four are directly related to the ability of an employee to deliver service in ways a client desires. These five are

1. The ability of employees to deliver service consistently, reliably, and accurately,

2. The willingness of employees to provide prompt, helpful service,

3. An employee's knowledge, courtesy, and ability,

4. An employee's willingness to provide individualized attention to each client, and

5. The appearance of the organization where employees deliver service. This research applies to HR staff as well.

The HR department's appearance is clearly influential in forming a client's impression of HR. However, the HR staff ultimately makes or breaks the department's reputation for client service. The reputation of the HR department is at risk in each and every HR staff-client encounter.

Remember the "moments of truth"? Everyone can recall a truly bad service experience that was caused by an indifferent, uncaring, discourteous, or disrespectful employee. One awful experience with HR can become for clients the moment of truth when they make a judgment on the overall quality of the HR staff. One unfortunate experience may overshadow the many other satisfying experiences that a client may have had with HR staff members. Experiencing a bad "moment of truth" may lead to a decision to minimize future interactions with HR and, worse, clients may tell others about the poor service the HR department delivers. Hiring client-centric people and training staff to deliver client-centric service all but guarantees that HR clients' "moments of truth" will be positive.

Hiring Client-Centric HR Staff

HR managers need to use a systematic process to identify people who are client-centric. There are several ways to do so.

Internal Employee Recruitment

Many HR departments promote from within because much of the training on the department's culture has already been done. Most internal candidates already know the HR department's beliefs and values, and they will have typically shown evidence of being comfortable or uncomfortable in that culture. The learning curve for new hires is reduced when the HR department hires from within the organization. Internal candidates already know what HR staff "really" believe in and reward. Moreover, HR managers typically have seen the employee perform on a daily basis. Hence, they already know the employee's skill, motivation, and commitment to client-centric service.

External Employee Recruitment

External job candidates should be recruited when existing employees have demonstrated that they are not capable or motivated to deliver client-centric service. Searching beyond the industry and dipping into service sectors makes excellent sense. Airlines often seek out and hire candidates from banks. Similarly banks hire people from hotels, and hotels hire people from restaurants. A discount financial brokerage service hired as many hospitality graduates from a business school as it could find once it discovered that these graduates understood business concepts and principles, and in addition knew how to deliver great client service. Manulife, a financial services company, replaced the retiring senior Vice President of Human Resources with its Vice President of Real Estate because she had not only business operations experience but also a reputation throughout the company for excellent client service.

KSAs of Client-Centric Staff

HR staff must have the interpersonal skills needed to relate effectively to clients and the creativity skills to resolve problems when they occur (for example, conflicting goals among clients). Manufacturing employees can be quite confident that each car on the assembly line will have essentially the same task requirements as every other car when it reaches their workstation. An assembly-line worker can also rely on the quality-control inspector to catch any errors before a car is shipped to a dealership. Not so in HR. HR staff must successfully perform their tasks with all types of clients who have all types of personalities — in the absence of a "quality inspector" to catch service mistakes before the client's experience is completed. HR staff must find and fix mistakes quickly, appropriately, and creatively when HR fails the client in some way. The nature and criticality of each client's judgment of the quality of each service experience make it essential to assess an HR applicant's attitude toward client-centric service before that person is hired.

Spotting Talent for Service

Former Chili's Chairman Norman Brinker said, "Look for people who are smart. Remember, sinners can repent, but stupidity is forever." At go!Mokulele Airlines in Hawaii, a receptionist was overheard telling a prospective employee on the phone, "You don't need specific qualifications to work here. You just need to be customer-focused."

Among the best predictors of performance in any job are cognitive ability and three personality dimensions that are good indicators of a client-centered disposition:

- » Conscientiousness: the extent to which a person is dependable and organized and perseveres on tasks
- » Agreeableness: the degree to which a person is amiable, tolerant, honest, cooperative, and flexible
- » Emotional stability: the degree to which a person is secure, calm, and independent and can work autonomously

The Situational Interview

When a large number of interviewers interview large numbers of candidates, consistency becomes both organizationally and legally important. A structured array of questions ensures that the interviewer collects the necessary personal and job-related data. It also assures uniformity in that every applicant is asked the same job-related questions derived from a job analysis, regardless of an applicant's age, race, sex, ethnicity, national origin, or religion.

A properly designed and administered situational interview means the questions are job-related, consistently scored, and asked of all candidates. Such an interview is a valid predictor of job performance.

Typically, a situational interview includes questions that address work competencies and service orientation. Candidates are presented with situations that contain a dilemma. The dilemma "forces" candidates to explain to an interviewer what they would do in a given situation rather than attempting to guess what the interviewers hope to hear (that is, give a socially desirable answer). The situational interview provides a revealing opportunity to evaluate what kind of service a candidate would likely deliver to clients in difficult situations.

An example of such a situational question might be the following: "As the new HR manager, you find your staff is constantly in conflict with clients. Many of the clients appear to have little respect for the expertise of your staff. The client who does appear to support HR in senior management meetings often insists that your staff do things that they know will not be effective. What would you do in this situation?"

Another question might deal specifically with hiring:

"You have been urged by a line manager to forego the standard hiring process because of time constraints? You also learn that the candidate the manager wants to hire is a former associate of the manager from another organization. Accommodating this request means not conducting a background check, a psychological evaluation, or a reference check — all part of your normal hiring process. You must decide what, as a client-centric manager, to tell this line manager. What would you do in this situation?"

A second group of questions that should be included in a situational interview relates to job competencies. Thus, an interviewer might assess the competence of an applicant for designing a monetary incentive program.

Service Skills in a Culturally Diverse Environment

Increasing numbers of employees come from diverse cultural and demographic populations. They expect that HR will understand their needs, values, and goals. Many large airlines hire multilingual flight attendants and reimburse attendants for taking language lessons. United Continental Holdings Inc., parent of United Airlines, offers classes for flight attendants in "Air Spanish," "Air Portuguese," and "Air Japanese." They learn the 40 or so words necessary to greet, board, and serve native speakers of these languages. They use a smile or culturally appropriate hand gestures for everything else. When the Opryland Hotel was preparing to host a large international meeting, it gave its 7,000 employees special training in international guest service. The grand training finale was an all-day international marketplace. Employees won prizes by participating in post-test games while dining on international foods.

A client-centric HR department must be sensitive to the needs of employees from varied backgrounds and lifestyles. This is because more than one in four people living in the United States is a member of racial or ethnic minorities, according to the Census Bureau. By 2015 the figure will be one-third. There is no longer a "typical" employee for whom the HR department can design one-size-fits-all selection, training, and reward systems. Dual-career couples, same-sex relationships, single mothers with child care responsibilities, and grown children with elder-care responsibilities are apt to be represented in an organization's workforce. Employing a diversified workforce, by tapping all available segments of the general labor pool, typically results in "the best" workforce. In a competitive environment, organizations must hire the best employees. The most successful organizations gain competitive advantage by seeking and recruiting talent wherever it may be found. With the increasing number of Baby Boomers retiring, the need for recruiting new employees grows daily. The point is that the HR manager must thoughtfully look in all parts of the available labor pool to find and recruit client-centric talent.

Employee Referrals

A straightforward way to hire client-centric employees is to ask your best employees to recruit them. These employees typically know your HR department's needs and values and what skills and attitudes are needed to perform well in meeting your HR department's mission. Moreover, they enjoy working for you, so therefore, they can be your best recruiters. HR staff who bring in friends feel responsible for their performance. They exert peer pressure on them to do well. Some HR managers pay a bonus to employees if they bring in a job candidate who stays through a probationary period. The reward might be monetary, or it could be a weekend trip to a resort area or dinner at a special restaurant.

Another option is to actively seek excellent employees who are already demonstrating service excellence elsewhere. Watching customer-contact employees do their jobs in the service industry is relatively easy. Every time you receive service or watch someone giving service either internally or externally, you can evaluate the server as a potential employee. Hiring people because you saw them working well elsewhere has the additional advantage of starting off the new relationship on excellent terms. Newly discovered employees are flattered that you recruited them. Asking people to consider a job opportunity in the HR department is an excellent way of "recognizing" them. Service expert Carl Sewell's philosophy is similar. The people he wants to hire are not out of work; they already have jobs. He recruits them by getting their friends to refer them to his Cadillac dealership because he believes that people who are truly good at providing outstanding service are probably friends of those who are also very good at doing this. The common belief in hospitality is "hire for attitude and train for job skills." While this is an effective strategy for hiring a restaurant server, it may seem like a stretch for HR with its expectation that qualified job candidates must have expert job knowledge and extensive educational training in HR management. Nonetheless, hiring those job candidates who have both HR expertise and a client-centric attitude is the only way for HR to become truly client-centric.

Becoming an Employer of Choice

An organization's reputation aids in recruitment. "Employers of Choice" have established a reputation for hiring and developing people for the long term. These organizations invest in their people, so they grow and develop; they keep their people challenged and motivated in their current jobs; and they offer them opportunities for advancement. Similarly, HR managers known for offering people a high-quality job and career opportunities attract high-quality applicants and build a pool of people who prefer to work for them rather than the competition. Gaylord Hotels is noted for offering growth and development opportunities to anyone who is willing to try. Because the company is known for living up to its commitment to employees, it not only wins annual "best place to work" awards, but it also seeks and gets a minimum of ten candidates for every job opening.

Southwest Airlines is an excellent example of how a company builds its brand as an employer by establishing an exceptional community reputation. In addition to providing multiple educational programs and opportunities that have earned the company renown for developing employees, Southwest spends time and money being a "good neighbor." It supports charity fund drives, gives to community organizations, and encourages its employees to be community volunteers. It employs people who enthusiastically tell their friends about the company. Even when the labor market is tight, Southwest has a deep labor pool. Everyone knows that the airline is a great place to work, not only for how Southwest treats its people as employees, but also for how it is respected as a good corporate citizen.

Training for Client-Centric Service

Once you have hired a candidate who has the necessary client-centric attitude, training begins. Providing at least 120 hours of training per employee each year, The Ritz-Carlton knows the value of ensuring that its employees have the knowledge, skills, and ability to deliver the high-quality service their customers expect. At the turn of the millennium, Federal Express was spending nearly 4.5 percent of its payroll annually on training employees. It invested nearly $70 million to build a totally automated education-certificate system that provides training to 40,000 couriers and agents in 700 locations. Holiday Inn Worldwide, part of the InterContinental Hotels Group, spends more than twice as much on training as most other hotel companies. The return on that training investment included a significant drop in customer complaints in some hotels from 200 per month to two or three, with a simultaneous revenue increase of 15 percent.

Client-centric HR departments face the challenge of training staff not only on required job skills, but also on how to interact positively with clients and on how to solve their problems creatively. A car going down the assembly line does not care if the autoworker has a bad attitude. However, the customer facing the bartender in a private club, the front-desk agent at the Four Seasons, or the ticket seller for a Broadway play certainly does. The same is true for HR clients. HR staff must be trained to provide caring service consistently. It goes far beyond the simple requirements of training someone to process a payroll, learn the union contract, or even become a strategic thinker. As an HR manager, you must train your team to master the art of client-centric service.

Visitors to Walt Disney World Resort assume employees will be consistently competent at the technical aspects of their jobs. In addition, they arrive with high expectations about the level of employee friendliness and enthusiasm. Street cleaners inside the Magic Kingdom quickly learn the mechanics of operating a pickup broom and dustpan. Learning the rest of the job, however, contributes far more to the ongoing success of Disney World. The street sweeper is, for many guests, the only available expert who knows where everything is located and the only person around to snap a group photo. He or she is also a constant reminder that the park is clean, safe, and friendly for all. To prepare that person properly for those multiple roles is an essential training task.

In addition to being taught HR's client-centric values and best practices, HR staff must know their client's objectives, values, and procedures, so they can be truly client-centric. This knowledge will help them figure out how to solve problems when a client is unhappy. Unless HR staff understand the values, beliefs, and mission of the HR department and its clients, in addition to its products and systems, they cannot know how to provide client-centric service. Because it is the client who defines the quality and value of the services provided by HR, staff must not only be experts in their functional areas, they must also learn their clients' business to become trusted business partners.

Service in Action: Gaylord Hotels

New employee training at Gaylord Hotels was designed to teach the culture, values, and job duties that are required learning for all new employees and to give them an idea of what the business of the company is. Gaylord's business strategy is to attract and retain groups holding meetings on a geographical rotation basis to draw the number of attendees needed to fill the sleeping rooms in each of their hotels. Thus, an association required by its national membership to meet around the country should find the Gaylord locations in Nashville, Orlando, Texas, and Washington, D.C., attractive. Because the hotels serve the meetings and convention business, the last day of orientation for new employees is a simulated convention with a registration desk, name tags, "goodie bags," breakout meetings in meeting rooms, plenary sessions, breaks, and a closing dinner. This simulation allows Gaylord to provide the necessary training to its new employees in the type of setting they will be operating in. Gaylord believes that employees who learn how it feels to be a convention attendee will be more successful in performing their jobs serving convention hotel guests.

The Big Picture

Teaching the "big picture" involves teaching HR staff the organization's overall values, purposes, and culture, and how HR helps the organization as a whole succeed. This is what Jan Carlzon did with SAS, and it paid handsome dividends for that organization. Once he told employees what they did that helped, or hurt, the organization's bottom line, they understood how their performance would add to, or detract from, the airline's success.

On the heels of his successful wall-to-wall service training program at SAS Group, Jan Carlzon instituted a second program. This follow-up initiative was designed to teach everyone in the organization how to read the company's financial statements. Jan believed that if all employees could understand these statements, they would better understand where the revenues came from, where the money went, how much it cost to run the company, and how much each employee could influence profit. The success of these wall-to-wall training efforts at SAS encouraged other organizations to train their entire workforce. British Airways followed suit by training all of its 37,000 employees in service. The lesson for HR is that to be, and to be seen as, a business partner, client-centric HR staff must be able to read and understand the financial statements of their clients.

New employees in any organization are usually eager to learn the organization's core values and understand its fundamental nature, so they can see how they fit into the big picture. Learning this information is especially beneficial in the HR department where its added value often exists in client perceptions. When HR staff are confronted with a problem situation that does not exist in a handbook or a training manual, the core cultural values learned and accepted during "big picture training" are what will lead each staff member to treat clients appropriately in unanticipated client-service situations calling for decisive action.

Multiple Training Processes

Using a variety of learning approaches keeps training from becoming dull. In addition to traditional classroom methods, an HR department can send staff out to observe exceptional organizations in the service industry with the goal of benchmarking against the best. HR can also sponsor book clubs to encourage staff to read about service excellence and to role-play a variety of on-the-job situations in which HR staff can practice the desired service skills. Because different people learn in different ways, this

---

Service in Action: NORPAC

Jim Taylor, the former Vice President of the HR Department at NORPAC, offers two training examples. The paper mill would send HR staff on sales calls to customers, so they could hear both kudos and complaints directly and, thus, get a sense of how NORPAC was performing as a business. The HR staff would bring that knowledge back to the mill to help set up training programs for production employees and for orienting new employees to NORPAC's values.

NORPAC's HR leaders innovated another program: The company created an "exchange" program in which production staff would periodically trade places with the customers NORPAC serves. For example, people from a newspaper pressroom would spend time working with NORPAC production people and vice versa. This experience was designed to give both sides a better appreciation of each other's needs in order to improve service. Taylor reported that "our people learned how the things that they do or don't do create pressroom problems, and pressroom people learned how they can be more specific in diagnosing problems when giving feedback to the mill. The result is a win-win for both."

variety of experiences facilitates learning. The HR staff can use its training expertise not only to develop innovative training methods and programs for teaching its own staff client-centric skills, but also to incorporate those innovations in training for all topics and departments.

Training Techniques

One-on-One Training

Southwest Airlines pairs new staff with veteran employees who know how to provide good service. According to Kevin and Jackie Freiberg, the co-authors of *Nuts: Southwest Airlines' Crazy Recipe for Business and Personal Success*, new customer-relations representatives undergo a four-week learning-by-example process.

"To start, they get first-hand experience in ground operations. They spend time with the customer service agents selling tickets, issuing boarding passes, tagging bags — doing all the things involved in customer service at the airport. When the new reps return to the Customer Relations Department, they don't just read a standard training manual cover to cover; instead, they team up with senior reps for the next phase of watching and doing. The first week, they listen to the senior people talk on the phone and watch them use the computer system for online research necessary to assist customers. The next week they start learning the computer while they continue to listen to the more experienced reps handle incoming calls. Finally, the employee team reverses roles."

Many HR professionals benefit from their SHRM regional associations. Through meetings, phone calls, blogs, and online chats, they can tap into an enormous pool of knowledge about how to deliver HR services. These opportunities typically include one-on-one learning as HR professionals communicate directly with a network professional. Together they find ways to solve problems, identify industry trends, and acquire the skills needed to adapt effectively to a changing workplace. It is the ultimate one-on-one training for professionals.

Training Technology

Many HR skills can be taught by one-on-one contact with a computer or web based program that simulates client encounters that a new HR staff member can expect to face. An HR manager can teach staff how to handle line managers' complaints or how to coach an appraisal interview by using a computerized simulation with an interactive software program. For example, a video may display an irate manager and then lead the HR trainee through the complaint-resolution process by letting the trainee take steps to resolve the complaint followed by showing the trainee the outcomes of these decisions. After the trainee chooses a response by touching the screen at the designated decision point, a video can show what happens after that choice has been made.

Federal Express uses DVDs, updated monthly, in more than 700 locations as the core of its automated educational certification system. Using this system, the company offers skills upgrading for any employee who needs it. Employees are given four hours of company-paid study and preparation time and two hours of self-administered tests. Airlines use sophisticated flight simulators to teach their pilots how to fly different airplanes into different airports and how to prepare for emergency situations. They create a virtual airplane with all the controls, physical layout of a cockpit, and simulated motions so that pilots flying the simulator feel as if they really are flying an aircraft. Pilots learn without putting the customers at risk. Learning to do something without putting oneself or the HR department's reputation at risk is a key advantage of a simulated experience. Simulations allow HR employees to practice their responses repeatedly until performance meets desired standards.

Even more engaging than virtual-reality simulations are interactive training opportunities available through Internet-based networks. Streaming video, webinars, and podcasts allow interaction between instructors and trainees anywhere in the world. Expertise can be delivered 24/7, anywhere to anyone online. Google and other search engines let learners access knowledge anywhere on the Internet: at certain university libraries, through HR networks such as SHRM, or even through the company's own knowledge-based system. As Google has become a verb, it confirms the power of the Internet to instantly find information on any topic.

The Internet has also revolutionized HR training and development programs in a globalized economy in which organizational clients are multiunit and geographically dispersed. Getting people to an educational center or a centralized training program can be difficult and is often not cost-effective. Getting these same people to log onto a training website is comparatively easy, and the amount of information, knowledge, and training they can obtain through this medium is enormous. Internet capabilities make just-in-time education a reality, as the people needing training can log onto the appropriate site at exactly the time they need it.

Retraining

Disney uses retraining programs for employees who experience burnout, who become unable to perform their current jobs because they lack the necessary technological skills, or whose jobs have been eliminated. A retraining program for burned-out employees can "sprinkle pixie dust" on employees who have become disenchanted with their present jobs or have otherwise lost their enthusiasm, recharging them with a renewed outlook. In the program, these employees can retrain for new jobs that will recapture their enthusiasm or allow them the opportunity to reflect on why they are unhappy with their existing jobs. The goal is for employees to regain the spirit of doing their job in ways that "wow" Disney's guests.

Cross-Functional Training

Cross-functional training augments HR staff members' capabilities, teaching them to perform a range of different jobs. The Opryland Hotel cross-trains its front-desk personnel and telephone-reservation operators so that each can help the other if necessary. The front desk, for example, often needs help when a number of people wish to check in or out within a short period of time. The hotel has set up a separate registration desk in the lobby, and when the line at the front desk reaches unacceptable limits, these cross-trained operators are called to the separate desk to help serve customers. Since all hospitality organizations have such variable demand patterns, cross-training is often necessary to handle the sudden surges in customers at different points in the service delivery system. At the same time, cross-training provides employees with task variety, and generates higher levels of engagement as a result, which in turn has significant benefits in increasing employee motivation and morale. Cross-training is clearly a win-win-win situation for the Opryland Hotel, its customers, and its employees.

To encourage the HR staff to be responsive to clients, client-centric HR departments offer cross-training for HR staff to learn the strategies, objectives, and cultural values of client departments across the organization. Cross-trained HR staff add capacity to specific HR functions when increases in demand for those services occur (for example, campus recruiting visits). Knowing that other HR employees can help out will only enhance a sense of team unity within HR. In addition, HR staff become welcomed "partners" when they go to their respective clients' departments. When HR staff can knowledgeably participate in a discussion of the merits of an operating department's strategy, it sends a strong message to this client that HR is truly client-centric. Virda Rhem, a SHRM Board member and Director of HR for Texas Property and Casualty Insurance Guaranty Association, suggests cross-training HR staff with the departments they serve to ensure that they get a better idea of what these departments do and how HR can better support their needs, wants, and expectations. Walking a mile in someone else's shoes not only allows you to gain a deeper understanding of what walking in those shoes means; it also allows you to earn the respect of the client in whose shoes you are walking. You show your willingness to do what it takes to enable your clients to achieve their strategic objectives.

Get In, Move Up: The Total Development Package

Remember, your competitors will always seek to hire your best — not your worst — people. Ignoring the needs of your HR staff to grow and develop may be an inexpensive short-run strategy, but it will become a long-run expense. Not giving staff opportunities to grow and develop may make it impossible for HR as a department to grow and develop. Having stellar hiring processes does the HR manager no good if the best employees needed for the department's future find better opportunities elsewhere to use their talents. The main idea behind training and development is that once you hire the best employees, they must be allowed to continue to grow in your organization. Skill and knowledge development — with a focus on client-centric service — is a continuous process that must be ongoing for organizational survival.

Chapter Takeaways

1. Look for and hire employees with a propensity for delivering client-centric service.
2. Conscientiousness, agreeableness, and emotional stability are three key qualities that signal a person's desire to deliver great service.
3. Recruit creatively from all demographic groups.
4. Assess commitment to a service orientation and test for it in job applicants using a situational interview.
5. Look for evidence of creative problem-solving ability.
6. Champion the training and development of your staff.

Chapter 6.

Motivating and Empowering Client-Centric Service

"We're not in the coffee business serving people; we're in the people business serving coffee."
— Howard Schultz, CEO, Starbucks

"Leaders think about empowerment, not control."
— Warren Bennis, Professor, University of Southern California

A family was checking in at the Hyatt Regency Grand Cypress on a busy night. The hotel was full; the family's reservation had not been properly handled, and the husband, wife, and three tired children were understandably upset. The front-desk agent assessed the situation and acted promptly. She took some quarters out of the petty cash drawer and gave them to the kids to play video games. She gave the parents chits for a drink in the lobby bar, while she went to find a manager to straighten out the problem. The parents were happy, and so were the kids. The front-desk agent had effectively defused a tense situation.

At the Imperial Hotel in Tokyo, a server overheard two customers talking about their college reunion. In Japan, college reunions occur yearly and usually have a good turnout. The server realized that college reunions were an untapped source of business for the hotel. He brought the idea up at the weekly meeting of his workgroup. Not long after, the hotel introduced a new package geared toward the reunion crowd. It was a huge success, bringing in $600,000 in revenue in the first two months.

These employees did not take a creative path to solving a customer problem because they were required to do so. The front-desk agent did not have a handbook that told her exactly what to do when a guest's reservation was lost. The server at the Imperial Hotel was not responsible for identifying new market opportunities. Those two employees were motivated to explore creative possibilities and new ideas, and to pass them along for development. The challenge for HR managers is not only to discover what makes HR staff do their jobs efficiently and competently, but also to learn what makes employees want to go the extra mile in serving their clients.

This chapter focuses on *motivating and empowering* HR staff as individuals and as a team to provide client-centric service. Since the quality of HR's service is ultimately defined by HR's clients, the HR staff member who interacts with any client must be well trained, and in addition highly motivated to meet the client's expectations consistently. If the HR department wants to be respected and valued throughout the organization, the HR manager must have the leadership and managerial skills to inculcate client-centric attitudes and motivate client-centric behaviors in the staff.

Because predefining all policies and procedures for handling any and all client interactions is not possible, HR staff must be empowered to handle the sundry situations that come up in the client interactions for which they are responsible. This skill is vital to an HR department's success. An HR manager must motivate staff members to do their jobs with creativity and enthusiasm. But how?

HR Staff Satisfaction and Client Satisfaction: A Direct Relationship?

J. Willard Marriott Jr., chairman of Marriott International, said, "It takes happy employees to make happy customers." It turns out there is scientific evidence that supports his claim. Ben Schneider, a past president of the Society for Industrial and Organizational Psychology, has conducted extensive research showing that satisfied employees make for satisfied customers, and satisfied customers can, in turn, reinforce employees' job satisfaction. Unless HR staff are happy performing their jobs, client satisfaction is difficult to achieve. The key to ensuring that HR staff are happy is to make sure they have the resources, training, and mandate to do their jobs well — and that they are rewarded fairly for doing so. If you as an HR manager offer appropriate training, incentives, and resources and fulfill your staff's needs, then they will not only be productive in their work, but they will be happy performing it. This is because people enjoy doing what they do well. If HR staff believe they are appreciated, then they are much more likely to treat their clients with appreciation as well.

How do you find out if your HR staff are satisfied? The Center for Creative Leadership recommends surveying employees several times a year on job aspects that typically affect job satisfaction, such as employee relationships with superiors, task variety, recognition, opportunities to learn and grow on the job, and autonomy. As reported in the *Wall Street Journal*, Sears, Roebuck and Co. studied attitudes of employees in 800 stores and found that attitudes about workload and how their bosses treated them had "a measurable effect on customer satisfaction and revenue. Sears found that a happy employee will stick with the company, give better service to the customer, and recommend company products to others." If employee attitudes improved by 5 percent, customer satisfaction improved by 1.3 percent, and revenue improved by 0.5 percent. If Sears executives "knew nothing about a store except that employee attitudes had improved 5 percent, they could reliably predict a revenue rise of 0.5 percent over what it would otherwise have been."

Mel Asbury, a former member of SHRM's Board of Directors, is the former Senior Vice President of Human Resources for Talecris Biotherapeutics Inc., SpectraSite Communications Inc., and Novant Health and the former Corporate Human Resources Manager for Exxon Mobil and GlaxoSmithKline. In each position, he encouraged his HR teams to regularly ask managers and employees across the organization for feedback. He used this information in creating the surveys he sent annually to clients to assess their satisfaction with the HR department's performance. The survey was available online to any employee anytime. By reminding his staff to ask clients for feedback, he reinforced their awareness of the client-centric philosophy he wanted to promote in HR. The feedback his staff received helped him greatly in deciding which HR programs were needed and which ones needed to be changed. In addition, the online "anytime surveys" provided instant, regular feedback regarding issues clients were experiencing with the service that the HR staff provided them.

Motivation for Client-Centric Service

Although everyone knows the value of money as a motivator, few know that most employees are also concerned with four other aspects of their jobs. The job must be fun, fair, interesting, and meaningful for them. Walt Disney said, "You don't work for a dollar — you work to create and have fun." Chili's Norman Brinker said, "If you have fun at what you do, you'll never work a day in your life. Make work like play, and play like hell." The key to managing and retaining client-centric employees is to successfully build these four elements into HR jobs.

Expected Outcomes

The first step to having highly satisfied HR staff who in turn will be motivated to satisfy clients is to clarify the relationship between what HR staff do and the outcomes they can expect. Most HR employees begin their jobs with energy and enthusiasm. They do not take a job to fail; they want to do well. But this desire may not last if they do not learn what they need to do to earn the appreciation of clients. They must see the relationship between their performance and the desired outcomes they can expect (for example, recognition). If the outcomes they can expect are not desired (for example, ongoing criticism from an impossible-to-satisfy boss), and if the outcomes they anticipate (such as the opportunity to learn new jobs and to grow) are the same for low performers as they are for high performers, their energy and enthusiasm will quickly dissipate. The keys to motivation are needs, values, goals, rewards for goal attainment, and characteristics of the job itself.

Meeting Staff Needs

People join one organization versus another to fulfill their needs. Though the needs of people vary, they usually include financial security, belonging to an organization that is aligned with their values, associating with people who think and feel the same way toward client service, growth and development as a person and as an employee, understanding clearly what is expected of them in their job performance, and feeling appreciated for meeting, or exceeding, those expectations.

Values and Goals

HR employees must believe that the HR department's client-centric values are consistent with their values. This belief is related to whatever reasons an employee had for affiliating with the HR department in the first place. If adhering to an HR policy is inconsistent with an individual's values, the policy will likely be ignored. If the policy is totally inconsistent with values that are important to an HR staff member, and the directive or policy cannot be ignored or avoided, that individual will probably resign from the HR department.

In addition to values, the HR staff must believe an HR policy is consistent with the HR department's client-centric values. An airline flight attendant, for example, noticed that the floor around the exit to her airplane was covered in oil, endangering the safety of deplaning passengers. The pilot directed the attendant to allow the passengers off the plane anyway. Because so many training sessions had stressed the primary importance of passenger safety, and without a reasonable explanation for departing from safety standards, the attendant ignored the pilot because the pilot's directive was clearly inconsistent with the organization's goals and the cultural values she had learned. If a directive or policy appears to conflict with an organizational goal, policy, tradition, or past practice, an HR manager must explain why this time "things are different."

Measurement and Rewards

Rewarding the wrong behavior is arguably as big a mistake as not rewarding the right behavior. An organization's reward and recognition system needs constant and careful review to make certain that the behaviors being rewarded are the behaviors that the organization desires. HR managers should avoid the common folly of telling people to do one thing while rewarding another. For example, the authors know a hotel that tells its employees they should make every effort to satisfy the guest. But the hotel's management

Service in Action: Gaylord Hotels

Gaylord quarterly produces "All STARS" pep-style rallies to celebrate the company's top-performing employees. What makes these rallies extra special is that Gaylord's foundation is built on entertainment. The company knows how to entertain people; it has employees who have entertainment talent, and it uses those skills in its productions. There is strong competition among employees, known as STARS, to be selected to participate in All STARS rally programs. The company is committed to finding a way to use everyone's talents. Each rally is themed differently and is dependent on the messaging that management seeks to deliver to the employees concerning the business. These rallies publicly celebrate Gaylord's commitment to open communications, reinforcing the relevance of the company's evaluates and rewards employee performance only according to the budgeted numbers. Consequently, employees seeking rewards and recognition focus on the numbers rather than on guest satisfaction — to the detriment of the company's customer service reputation. Similarly, if the HR department stresses its commitment to being client-centric but does not reward those who practice it, the HR staff will quickly see that being client-centric does not count for much.

The Ritz-Carlton and other leading hospitality organizations that constantly and consistently remind employees of the significance of service excellence celebrate employees' successes in customer service, and they do so visibly and publicly. As an example, when a customer writes a letter to the company telling about what a wonderful job an employee did in providing an outstanding customer experience, the manager of that employee's department will read the letter during a department meeting and bring pizza or ice cream to mark the occasion.

values and highlighting the fun that employees have doing their jobs.

Gaylord celebrates successes of individual contributors by selecting hotel STARS who best represent each of its seven values. STARS are selected by a committee composed of former winners. A three-minute video is prepared on each person and shown at the rally along with the awarding of a plaque. These are emotionally charged events that make the STARS feel valued, recognized, and appreciated while teaching all who attend what the company values, recognizes, and appreciates. Winners of the coveted "Value" award are company "heroes" honored by being included in the Value Wall of Fame, which chronicles the stories of Value award recipients over the years. The award is a powerful tool in teaching the company's values.

A maxim in organizational psychology and management is "that which gets measured gets done." Dysfunctional, nonclient-centric behavior can almost always be traced back to how HR staff perceive they are measured. The HR department must define with clients and staff what is meant by client-centric performance and then evaluate the staff accordingly.

Job Characteristics and Team Dynamics

A client-centric HR manager must start with a focus on the job environment to ensure it is properly enriched. Do HR staff have task variety and a chance to grow and develop, or are they stuck in a routine doing the same things day in and day out? Are they given autonomy to use their expertise and creativity, or are they constantly required to perform their jobs "by the book"? Are they empowered to do what they know how to do, or are they closely watched? Do responsibility and accountability rest largely with them or with you, their HR manager? To whom is recognition given for jobs well done — the HR staff member, the staff as a whole, or primarily you?

George Koenig, former senior human resources executive for Sodexo, stressed the importance of ensuring that everyone is on the same page. He stated that every organization needs someone to paint the broad picture and to constantly remind everyone of how all the parts fit together. An HR manager must frequently take the initiative to demonstrate the meaning of the big picture to HR employees to enable them to offer help to the right people at the right time — all with the goal of achieving the organization's mission. When Disney calls a group of people together to identify service quality problems and opportunities, they work hard on behalf of that group's goal because they are so committed to the goals of the Disney organization. If an HR manager empowers the HR staff to satisfy their needs, values, and goals, the HR manager will have the support of a client-centric staff.

One meaningful characteristic of a job is the opportunity to work with others in groups and teams. While groups allow people to fulfill their need to affiliate and to identify with like-minded others, a team goes further. Table 6.1 shows team characteristics that are required to support a collection of people to function successfully as a work team. The HR department can use these characteristics to help turn groups into teams, and to help less successful work teams thrive.

Table 6.1 Successful HR Team Characteristics

- Has a meaningful purpose that inspires and focuses team's efforts.
- Has goals and objectives that are specific, measurable, attainable, relevant, and have a timeframe.
- Is small enough to act as a cohesive team (typically 5-15 members).
- Has members with the necessary skills to operate as a team (functional/technical skills appropriate for the decision area, team process skills, problem-solving/decision-making skills, service skills).
- Has clear, well-articulated work norms and values that are enforced by the team.
- Has a cultural value of mutual accountability where only the team can fail or succeed: "We win as a team; we lose as a team."
- Is led by a team-building HR manager who creates and sustains a strong client-centric culture.

If HR staff have common needs, beliefs, values and goals, the team as a whole can monitor and oversee each member's performance. The HR team's approval usually has a greater influence on an employee's behavior than does an HR manager.

Mel Asbury, former Senior Vice President of Human Resources for several companies, set aside time at his weekly and monthly HR staff meetings to have team members present a report on what they had done on a major project that other team members might find interesting, or that might affect their work. "I found this helped greatly in breaking down barriers to teamwork and in addition providing recognition to staff members. They could also throw out issues that they were struggling with to gather team input." The result was "a great team with a sense of self-worth, the opportunity to grow and develop, a means to recognize and share achievements and failures, and a way to reinforce the team's values and beliefs."

Empowerment for Client-Centric Service

Shared decision-making at both the individual and team level leads to empowerment. Empowering employees to make decisions and to take initiative provides opportunities for growth and development for the team and the individuals in it. Moreover, it makes the job interesting. As Norman Brinker said, "You can achieve so much more by empowering people to achieve on their own. Don't be too hands-on." Empowerment is the assignment of a manager's decision-making responsibility to an individual or a group. It requires sharing sufficient information and organizational knowledge to enable an HR employee to understand and contribute to both the department's and the client's performance. It involves giving employees authority to make decisions that influence HR departmental and client outcomes. Empowerment can include decision-making responsibility for all or part of one's job.

Empowerment is also a mechanism by which responsibility for job-related decisions is vested either in individuals or in work teams.

Service in Action: Exxon Mobil

Mel Asbury tells the story of a junior employee who was assigned the task of employee wellness. While this job would normally be assigned to the head of benefits, he thought a junior member might be better able to relate to employees on the topic. As he states,

"To everyone's delight, she developed on her own a dynamic employee wellness program that changed the culture inside the organization, and all of it was done with very few resources or money. She identified many community resources that were free. We offered health risk appraisal, on-site screenings, Weight Watchers, exercise programs and others. She did a wonderful job!"

Empowerment means you as an HR manager must willingly share relevant information about, and control over, factors that affect your own job performance.

Empowerment is not an all-or-nothing issue. There can be degrees to which employees and groups are empowered to make decisions. If one thinks of decision-making as having different components (for example, finding problems, uncovering alternatives, evaluating alternatives, making choices, implementing a decision, and following up to see if it works), empowerment can include some or all of these components on some or all of the decisions a team makes. For example, a team could be entirely responsible for and empowered to identify a training problem, find alternatives for solving it, and even make and implement the best decision for solving it. Below are some of the different degrees of employee empowerment in action.

Participatory Empowerment

Participatory empowerment typically involves the creation of autonomous workgroups. These groups are given decision-making responsibility for issues related to both job content and job context. Such groups participate in problem identification, alternative search and analysis, and recommendations for the best choice in job content. The evidence suggests high job satisfaction and performance in these groups.

In the early 1990s, The Ritz-Carlton hotels set a goal: the revolution/transformation of hotel operations through the implementation of self-directed work teams (SDWTs). As described by The Ritz-Carlton, an SDWT is a group of employees responsible for the following:

- » Sharing leadership functions
- » Improving work processes
- » Developing team goals
- » Reviewing team performance
- » Coaching and training fellow team members

The Ritz-Carlton found that SDWTs increase accountability for the success of the business to the work teams who operate the business. These groups take responsibility for the quality of their products and services. SDWTs liberate and unleash the creative potential and entrepreneurial abilities of employees. At The Ritz-Carlton, implementing SDWTs resulted in an improvement in service quality and a subsequent rise in both customer and employee satisfaction. In addition, SDWTs freed managers from the day-to-day operational aspects of their jobs. Rather than working *in* the system, managers now have the time to work *on* the system, providing vision and direction.

Self-Management

Self-management for individuals involves giving employees decision-making authority. Giving HR staff this authority requires extensive employee involvement in the development of the HR department's vision, mission, and goals. Empowering a person or team to make decisions that optimally respond to changing environmental conditions, technological innovations, and competitive challenges is the ultimate expression of trust by an HR manager in the staff.

The benefits of empowering individuals include high productivity, high job attendance, low voluntary turnover, and improvements in both product and service quality.

Team Decision-Making

By involving the HR team in solving problems and making decisions, HR and the team gain the benefits of empowered individuals. The HR department learns more about what it wants to do and how to do it, and the individual HR team member learns more about HR's job, why the job is done the way it is, how other team members contribute to the department's goals, and the relationship of the strategy to the department's goals. Empowering HR staff in decision-making also enables

Service in Action: W. L. Gore and Associates

Self-management can be achieved with or without formally designated work teams. Gore and Associates, the manufacturers of Gore-Tex, has no titles, hierarchy, or any of the conventional structures associated with a company of its size and sales of approximately $1 billion a year. The company has been highly successful and profitable for more than 30 years, and growth has been financed without debt. With empowerment at Gore nearly total, employees have decision-making authority and responsibility for both job context and content. The culture and norms of the organization support employee empowerment. There is no fixed, assigned authority, and "associates" work in the absence of structure or management.

the HR manager to understand clearly the problems and issues confronting the department. After all, if HR managers do not know what they are trying to do, or why a particular issue is important, they cannot explain it to their staff, let alone to their clients. Furthermore, what better way to teach HR staff the reasons a job is done the way it is and the way each job impacts clients than by including staff in decision-making? What better way to show how an HR job helps others attain their goals than by involving staff in HR client-related decisions? Team decision-making empowers HR staff to become increasingly involved and accountable for their work.

Team decision-making has an additional benefit. When the team makes decisions, it owns them because it understands them. Just as an empowered employee gains ownership of decisions he or she makes, an empowered team gains ownership of the decisions it makes. Hence, the team becomes responsible for making its decisions work. If the quality team at a hotel decides that too many dishes are breaking on the food-service carts while running over the tiled floor, that team will likely find solutions. In this actual example, the team came up with the idea of putting rubber spacers between the trays. Since the quality team, made up of members who pushed the carts came up with the solution, the team members ensured they used the rubber bumpers in ways that proved their solution was a good one. Sadly, such problems are too frequently left for an "expert," such as an industrial engineer, to come up with a solution that nobody uses because it was "not invented here." The problem then continues, and frustrated managers wonder what to do in light of unresponsive employees.

Assigning Decision-Making: What Is Best for Your HR Department?

Empowerment begins by focusing on problems related to the job, then gradually moves through the various decision-making stages, from problem identification through implementation and follow-up. After HR staff, as well as you the HR manager, become comfortable with empowerment, increasing levels of empowerment can be added by raising the level of decision-making authority from problem identification up through implementation and follow-up. At each step, the HR manager determines what difficulties were created, how they should be addressed, and whether the individuals or teams are sufficiently trained and motivated to move to the next stage of decision involvement and responsibility. Alternatively, an HR manager might empower staff to address problem identification and development of alternatives simultaneously. For either of these approaches, HR managers first need to determine which decisions they would like to empower HR staff to make. Second, a plan must be developed to prove that HR staff members are ready, willing, and able to make the decisions with which they are charged. The HR manager has to decide what level of empowerment the staff is capable of doing and what can be done to implement that desired degree of involvement in making job-related decisions. In summary, the four chief requirements of a successful empowerment program are as follows:

1. Training in knowledge areas, decision-making, and group interaction.

2. Specific, measurable goals so that the empowered employees have a means to assess whether the decisions they made are good or bad in facilitating goal attainment. Moreover, HR managers need measures to monitor the quality of decisions made by empowered employees.

3. Methods of gauging progress toward goal attainment. People need yardsticks to see for themselves if what they are doing is heading them toward or away from the desired goals.

4. An incentive system to reward employees for appropriate client-centric decisions.

Why do you want to consider these steps for empowering your staff? Southwest Airlines former CEO Herb Kelleher noted the following:

"I can't anticipate all of the situations that will arise at the stations across our system. So what we tell our people is, 'Hey, we can't anticipate all these things; you handle them the best way possible. You make a judgment and use your discretion; we trust you'll do the right thing. If we think you've done something erroneous, we'll let you know — without criticism, without backbiting.'"

This philosophy that works so well for Southwest Airlines also works well for other benchmark service organizations that depend on their empowered employees to make the difference in the quality and value of service that their customers experience. They are the models for HR departments who strive to transform themselves into client-centric HR.

Chapter Takeaways

1. Discover not only what it takes to enable HR staff to do their jobs efficiently and competently, but what inspires them to go the extra mile in providing client-centric service.

2. Address the keys to motivating your staff: needs, values, goals, rewards for goal attainment, and characteristics of the job itself.

3. Reward behaviors you want, and do not ignore undesirable behaviors.

4. Show employees the relationships between their personal goals, HR departmental goals, and the organization's goals. Find win-win-win solutions.

5. Involve the HR team in solving problems and making decisions.

6. Empower your staff to the degree that makes sense given their training capabilities, and motivation.

7. Give people a chance to grow in their jobs, and then reward them for doing so.

Chapter 7.

Information Systems: Communicating Client-Centric Service

*"Communicate everything you can to your associates.
The more they know, the more they care."*
— Sam Walton, founder of Wal-Mart

A traveler was waiting for her breakfast to be served at a business hotel. Within a reasonable time, the server brought her eggs and bacon. She looked at the bacon and realized it was undercooked. She moved it to the side and proceeded to eat the rest of her meal. The manager came by and asked her about her breakfast. "Good," she said, "except the bacon was not cooked properly." The manager apologized and went on to another table. A short time later, the server appeared and asked her the same question. The traveler was now angry. Not only did the restaurant do nothing about the poorly cooked bacon, the manager did not even share the information with the server so that he would know of the problem.

"Innoventions" in Epcot had a big display by a major electronic game maker. Many different types of games were available to show the wonders of the technology and the exciting games this company had developed. A visitor walking through the display picked up the controls of one game. After mashing every button in an effort to make the game work, the visitor, unable to figure it out, walked away in frustration. The display provided no information, written or otherwise, for her.

Both situations illustrate the challenges of managing information. In the first case, although the information was available, the manager did not communicate it to the server to alert him about a customer's problem. Consequently, the server was unable to make the dining experience better, and the customer was left frustrated and angry. In the second illustration, the Epcot visitor was surrounded by information technology of the most advanced kind, but because the "right information" about how to work the game was unavailable, she could not figure out how to enjoy it.

Creating a system that manages information effectively is among the most challenging issues facing all HR departments. *Information* is data that informs, and an *information system* is a method to get that which informs to those who need to be informed. A well-designed information system delivers the right information to the right person in the right format at the right time so that it adds value to the person's choices.

The information system in a client-centric HR department has two principal components. First, it must provide HR clients with the information they need, when they need it, to make effective decisions. Second, it must supply information in the format and manner that clients want to find it. The manner in which the system delivers information should communicate to clients that "HR is providing this information in order to help you succeed in meeting your objectives." Thus, client-centric information systems not only attend to *what* information is provided but to *how* and *when* that information is delivered.

Information to Enhance Client-Centric Service

Since service is by definition intangible, the information that client-centric HR departments provide to their clients makes HR services tangible. This is one critical purpose of the information system. What information should HR provide? In what format, when, and in what quantity will the information help create the HR service experience that the client expects and wants? In the restaurant business, if the "experience" is dining in a formal setting, the restaurant should organize all the information it provides patrons to cue their perception that this is indeed a formal dining environment. The chef should have a clean white coat and a hat that signals, "I am a chef, not simply a cook. I have the skills and training to create a fine dining experience." The silverware and plates should be elegant. Everything in the environment should communicate the message "fine dining experience." Since some patrons do not have the refined taste necessary to judge an outstanding dining experience from the food alone, the restaurant must manage the many bits of information that the customer receives through all senses — what is tasted, touched, heard, seen, and smelled — to make certain that each one contributes to the perception of an elegant fine dining experience.

Communication Cues

Similarly, informational cues should communicate what an HR department wants to tell clients about the quality and value of its services. Information glues together the service product, the service setting, and the service delivery system to make a "whole" service experience. HR should use information technology to provide information in a way that makes the client experience seamless and satisfying. Satisfied clients, in turn, will repeatedly seek HR's services.

How an HR department delivers information through its information system cues a client's perception of how committed HR is to providing service. An HR department sends a powerful message when it provides information that was not requested yet clients find useful (for example, employment trends in needed skill areas). Likewise, HR can offer unrequested, yet welcomed services to employees on career planning (for example, suggest to specific employees job opportunities that fit their career goals and experiences; notify employees of training opportunities). HR can even develop a system for signaling a client when problems are likely to arise, such as when voluntary attrition is trending upward. In these examples, HR goes beyond informing clients on day-to-day changes in laws, HR policies, and employment regulations — the basics that HR managers know they must cover to help their clients achieve their goals — and provides additional information to help clients be proactive, innovative, and a step ahead of potential problems. HR's responsibility is to manage information systems to ensure not only that those who need HR information receive it in a timely fashion, but that helpful, decision-related knowledge is readily accessible to help clients attain their goals. Acting on these and other opportunities shows a commitment to client-centric service.

It's not just about the content and structure of the information system that is important. It is also how HR communicates that sends a message to clients about how committed the department is to service. Medical doctors hang their diplomas on the wall; restaurants display food reviews; and hotels display their American Automobile Association ratings — all in an effort to say to customers, "Your experience will be a good one."

Even sensory information should be managed to communicate a message about what the client's experience with the HR department should be like. That message should be consciously and carefully defined by the HR staff. For example, empathetic listening skills, uncluttered workstations, and easy, open access to HR staff communicate to a client, "We are happy you are here, and we are ready to assist you." HR staff actions send a message, for good or for ill. For example, when HR staff go onto the production floor to talk to hourly employees or visit a manager's workspace, they send a strong message about how they value clients' opinions and time.

For clients too remote for HR staff to visit, attention should be paid to access portals. As George Koenig, former senior HR executive for Sodexo, noted from his experience in providing HR services to geographically dispersed employees, it is important to communicate the same client-centric service to those you cannot meet face to face as you do to those with whom you can talk one on one. This approach puts enormous emphasis on the HR access portal employees use, whether it is a web interface or an HR direct contact. When a client contacts the HR department with an issue, HR staff must authentically communicate a spirit of genuine helpfulness that can be felt long-distance. Requiring clients to confront a confusing and long automated telephone tree only frustrates them, as will an endlessly ringing phone followed by voice mail. Good service communicated over the phone can go a long way toward conveying the HR department's respect for clients and their needs. A confusing, outdated, unattended, or dysfunctional Internet portal or cumbersome telephone tree make it likely that distant clients will get frustrated, "click off" or hang up, and avoid seeking HR's help in the future. Even when the budget may favor technology at the portal, a client-centric HR manager will consider the impact of a busy signal, call transfers to voice mail, or other cues of unavailability on client perceptions of HR. If clients think the HR department is unresponsive, it will be viewed negatively regardless of "good" statistics on average response times.

Systems Tailored to the Client

A client-centric information system must consider not only the "what" but the "how," "when," and "where." Thus, the information system should be designed to integrate HR's service product (its expertise) and the system by which it delivers its service product. An integrated information system provides accurate and current information to both HR staff and their clients when they need it. Doing this well requires understanding the needs and expectations of the users in terms of their capabilities and their willingness to use the information. Providing 30 pages of statistical output to a person who does not understand statistics or who does not have the time to sort through pages of data to find the needed information is not helpful. If you are out of pasta in your restaurant, you do not want to take the time to find and review statistical predictions of how much pasta you were supposed to use this week, or the sales forecast for next week, or the summary data for last week. You want to find someone who can get more pasta to the restaurant immediately. Likewise, if an HR client is in desperate need of employees now, showing the client a manpower planning chart does the client nor HR any good.

Information as Product

One of the most effective strategies for providing the right information at the right time is to give employees access to an HR website that interfaces with a client database. Sending masses of information through traditional organizational communication channels can be time-consuming and frustrating. Information centralized in an online database helps employees find exactly what they want quickly. The information then becomes a tangible and

Service in Action: FreshPoint

FreshPoint, a division of Sysco Corp., offers a good illustration of the benefits of a sophisticated information system. This wholesale grocer — which sells more fresh fruits and vegetables to central Florida restaurants, hotels, theme parks, and other hospitality customers than all of its competitors combined — knows that information can be as valuable a product for customers as its fresh produce. FreshPoint developed an information system that enables it to accurately predict what customers will need and when they will need it. In effect, FreshPoint has moved beyond the business of fruits and vegetables into the business of managing customer inventories. Its computer models are so powerful that FreshPoint frequently knows better than its customers not only what they need, but when. Fruits and vegetables are extremely perishable and require easily deliverable product. A simple tool for making information readily available online is HR's use of social networking through which staff can disseminate information almost instantaneously to everyone on the list with computer access. While the information is necessarily limited in these one-way communications, the instant deliverability makes for an excellent tool for communicating changes in policy, the availability of new resources and services, and updates on HR current issues.

Organizations use various informational techniques such as directional signs or symbols to help people find their way. Disney and Universal, for example, use themes to orient their customers as to where they are physically in the Magic Kingdom or Universal Studios. Internet portals likewise should use "wayfinding" techniques such as familiar symbols and words to guide people to the right web page. The website for a client-centric HR department should have the capability to help clients find the forms and

lead time to obtain from often distant growers. Having this information system allows FreshPoint to deliver the freshest products to its customers for service to serve their restaurants because FreshPoint tracks their past usage patterns, predicts future usage, and then manages their current inventory carefully.

Through the capabilities of this information system, FreshPoint has become responsible for the freshness and availability of fresh fruits and vegetables for its restaurant customers. One large restaurant operation no longer even bothers to do its own ordering. Instead, it has essentially outsourced that function by allowing FreshPoint to generate orders automatically via an EDI (Electronic Data Interchange). FreshPoint makes certain that fresh produce is in the restaurant ready to use when it is needed instructions for conducting performance appraisals, handling employee discipline, and performing other HR functions. Beyond these functional items, however, a client-centric HR department might add extra help for clients, including streaming video on how to coach employees or to interview job candidates, as well as on-demand videos that offer training in functional skills, orientation for new employees, or a recap of the CEO's discussion of the organization's year-end-review report.

When one company needed help managing its employees' learning and training, it found a learning management system on the software as service (SAS) model. In this model, the vendor hosts and maintains the software, keeps it updated, and handles security. The company then uses the SAS to help it manage its learning activities in a cost-effective way. These systems allow the company to manage its training and educational records, distribute courses virtually, and offer online collaboration among its learners. The company's training officer claimed that if he did not have this technology, he would have required six or seven additional people to offer the company's employee development activities.

In other words, when information is the service, client centricity is a function of how easy it is to access and how helpful it is in enabling clients to co-produce HR responsibilities. HR departments valued for their client focus go beyond basic functional tasks and provide useful supporting information to their clients. They anticipate a client's informational needs and then make the right information available when it is needed. For example, HR can create programs that notify a manager when a department's employee accident rate exceeds the norm for the industry and suggest ways that a department's manager can promote safe behavior.

Today, HR departments have access to a variety of impressive applications for their information systems. For example, online succession planning and performance appraisal systems walk the client through the processes and provide instant help at every stage. Information systems can even automatically monitor the process to check that these functions are performed in a timely way with all the needed steps completed. For employees, information systems can personalize their HR service. The University of Central Florida's myUCF online portal allows employees to access their individual benefits account and make changes in their preferences at any time.

But as noted above, these applications of technology are only a starting point. As is true of any procedure designed to improve service to customers, HR needs to assess the relationship between the value and the cost of the information before it establishes such a system. Because professional chefs at fine dining restaurants think of themselves as artists and not accountants, they may not get around to gathering and organizing data about ingredient supplies frequently enough to justify the expense of a complex online system. If the input of data is haphazard, the value of out-of-date information would be low and the expense of installing an advanced system unwarranted. Thus, HR should use technology intelligently, delivering service that clients may not have known they needed but, once available, is recognized by them as both useful and cost-effective.

Information as Relationship Marketing Tool

"Relationship marketing," or marketing to a "segment of one," is now possible through the increasing power of customer relationship management (CRM) software. Computers can store, digest, and interpret large quantities of information that are client-specific. When customers return warranty cards on products, fill out the information on cents-off coupons, click on a website, or send in for free premiums such as T-shirts and company-logo coffee mugs, they provide information (or tracking "cookies") that organizations use to increase their understanding of the individual needs of their customers. If you search for a book online at Amazon.com, the electronic bookstore lets you know about new books on the same subject the next time you visit the website. Taking it a step further, social networking websites pay attention to your likes and dislikes, the language in which you write, your geographical location, and other information to tailor the ads you see to reflect your interests.

Similarly, by carefully collecting and mining data, an HR department can store and organize extensive knowledge of all of its client's needs, wants, and actual behaviors. Data analyses then enable HR to identify both individual and group client tendencies, trends, and patterns so that it is able to respond to those quickly

---

Service in Action: The Ritz-Carlton

The Ritz-Carlton hotels provide an excellent customer experience partly because their information system collects data that allows employees to provide customers with more than just a clean room. The Ritz-Carlton's definition of a properly prepared room includes having service providers check the information system to review items that the day's incoming customers have indicated in previous stays are important to them. They know from previously gathered information that certain customers expect to find extra pillows, hot chocolate, or specific magazines in their rooms. The Ritz-Carlton database tells the hotel the preferences of each repeat customer, so the hotel can be sure that the desired items are in the room when a customer arrives.

The Ritz-Carlton also asks employees to gather and share information related to enhancing service delivery. Employees are asked to listen for and record in the database any relevant customer-related information that might assist The Ritz-Carlton in adding value and quality to the customer's experience. For example, if a floor sweeper overhears a couple talking about celebrating their anniversary, the sweeper passes the information along so that the hotel can take notice of this special event. The employees help deliver a memorable Ritz-Carlton experience by inputting useful knowledge into the organization's information system.

and, sometimes, to even respond before the clients themselves recognize a need for HR services. That is client-centric service.

Information in the Environment

Informational features provided by an HR department in the work environment can range from a simple orientation map that tells new employees where they are physically located, to elaborate website designs that allow clients to easily access interactive computerized information systems to use HR services. Epcot offers information that characterizes and enhances the service setting. At the theme park's Innoventions area, monitors are located in highly visible locations, allowing customers to check on the availability of dinner reservations at the park's many dining locations. By going through a menu of options, a park visitor can learn if the Mexican, French, or Moroccan restaurants have available seating capacity at the desired time; if so, the customer can electronically make a reservation for that time. Epcot also has a WorldKey Information Service designed to answer frequently asked questions about the park. This environmental feature provides specific information about the park's different services and can even be accessed via an application on smart phones. In addition, it serves as a symbol of the advanced technology that the entire Epcot Innoventions environment is designed to portray.

In this high-tech world, technology can take over many functions previously performed by employees. As a result, and perhaps ironically, nearly everyone values a high-touch experience more than ever. Few people really want to talk to a telephone tree. Service organizations such as The Ritz-Carlton therefore try to use as much technology behind the scenes as they can to save on labor costs so they can afford enough front-of-the-house staff to offer the personal contacts and touches that impress customers. HR can design its information system to deliver the same brand of client-centric service as The Ritz-Carlton by automating those functions that do not directly impact clients, or those they do not see. The "human touch" should be made available where the client needs and wants it.

Informing the HR Staff

Basic as it may seem, HR managers also need to provide their own staff with information that allows them to understand how HR can best serve clients and to make decisions to that end. An internal information system should be designed to ensure that HR staff have the "back of the house" information they need to serve clients well. Providing HR staff with the right information at the right time in the right format so they can satisfy and truly impress organization managers is as crucial as the external information system is to those managers and their employees.

How should HR's internal information system work? Consider an HR staff member who must decide whether to redesign or replace a compensation program that is being rendered obsolete by changing labor market conditions. The HR staff member will need data about optional programs at benchmarked companies, costs and benefits of those programs, and the compiled concerns and recommendations of

Service in Action: Disney

Disney's daily count system offers a good illustration of how an information system can be designed to inform staff on decisions for improving client experiences. In the daily count, every customer entering a Disney park is counted and added to the total in the park at that time. Based on its extensive attendance database and knowledge of arrival-rate distributions, Disney is able to predict after the first hour of operation how many customers will come into each park during the entire day. This number is used to inform the food and beverage people how much food needs to be taken from central storage facilities and brought into each park's various restaurant and food-service locations and how many salads, soups, and other prepared food items need to be on hand.

Further, since Disney now knows how many guests will be coming into the park that day, these data are managers and their employees within the organization. Each piece of information represents the end product of some HR staff member's efforts and should be available in the HR information system. When the system is not designed to accommodate the information needs of its own people, there will be an internal service failure by the HR department to its own staff. Moreover, if HR has not organized the information-gathering responsibilities of its staff, how can it do its job of disseminating the information to managers and employees across the organization, informing everyone what they need to know?

The entire movement toward employee empowerment that characterizes client-centric HR departments depends on HR staff members having easy access to the information they need to provide exceptional client-centric service. Without a systematic way to accomplish this goal, staff empowerment is impossible. HR staff must have access to information to help clients make insightful decisions, operate successfully, and assess the results of their decision-making activity on HR issues and activities across the organization.

made available to human resource managers to verify that the proper number of employees is scheduled to handle the expected number of customers. Similarly, the supervisors and area managers of the various attractions access these data to know how many cars, boats, and trains need to be available for their attractions. In short, the first-hour customer count informs a number of pertinent decision areas so that the parks are prepared to serve all the day's customers with the level of service quality that Disney strives to provide — and that customers expect. This one data source, flowing through the information system, is used simultaneously to improve the quality of the service itself, the service environment, and the service delivery system. The information generated by the system improves customer experiences and does so with high efficiency.

As in the Disney example, HR can introduce high-tech human resource information systems (HRIS) to collect and distribute information that HR staff need to perform their functions. HRIS keep track of payroll, employment, employee qualifications, training, discipline, administration of routine record-keeping for performance reviews, and the many other areas essential to the management of an organization's human resources. Client-centric HR departments can use this powerful software to track their employees in the same way Disney tracks its guests and can allow its clients to access these data in making decisions about such things as departmental salary levels, future employment needs, and employee development.

Advanced Information Systems

Information systems range on a continuum from a simple provision of basic information to the most sophisticated artificial intelligence. Two key types of systems that do more than simply provide information are decision support systems and expert systems. Decision support systems are those that collect data and then assist a manager by providing the right information at the right time using a preprogrammed decision rule. Expert systems are more advanced in that the rules can be used in lieu of a manager. While decision support systems support managers making choices, expert systems go further by actually making choices automatically from available alternatives. In general, the decision support systems pertain to "if/then" situations that assist a manager, while expert systems apply to two kinds of situations, one being a decision rule that is used in lieu of a manager, and the other being a contingency approach that accommodates a computer program to make "it depends" decisions. Advanced forms of expert systems where the situations are so ambiguous that hard and fast rules do not always apply are sometimes called artificial intelligence. More details about these information systems follow.

Decision Support Systems

Decision support systems, as the name implies, contain decision rules that help a person make a decision. An example is an automatic warning that signals a manager when an inventory level of a critical product is low or an icon that flashes on a computer screen to warn a cruise-ship engineer that a piece of equipment is heating up. In HR, a decision support system can be as simple as a reminder to a client that a performance review needs doing. More elaborate applications allow a client to make appropriate HR decisions. For example, an HR program can guide a client through the steps for hiring, since this process can be accurately modeled. In these cases, an information system provides a flow of information to a decision-maker who can then use that information to respond when the monitored information indicates that a decision should be made.

Decision support models can be built when an organization has learned that certain relationships are always, or nearly always, true. If a pressure sensor in a Tunnel of Love ride at a theme park registers a certain amount of weight and the weight changes mid-ride, the ride triggers an alarm to the ride operator to shut it down because someone has likely left the car and started walking on the track. Since this behavior is very dangerous, the information system is programmed to check the weight sensor constantly. Other illustrations of the use of information that can support a client in decision-making can be seen in recommendations for reorders of merchandise when stocks are low, staffing levels for a predicted high-demand period, quantities of certain foods based on statistical projections, or notifications to a control tower manager to send out a search team for an overdue airplane. An HR example may be found in an application that tracks the performance of an employee and signals to a supervisor when a required goal-setting or feedback session is needed. Given the legal protocol that must be followed regarding employee discipline, an HR information system can track whether the proper procedures in that process were followed — as well as provide a record for legal purposes.

The decisions in the above examples can be modeled because the environment in which they occur is relatively predictable. Since these decisions also occur frequently, developing a mathematical model describing the situation is often worth an HR department's time. As we will see in further detail below, an organization can take the decision support system used in guiding managers in relatively predictable and routine decisions and transform these into an automatic decision mode. A restaurant, for example, that needs to keep track of the canned food inventory can build a model that automatically recognizes when the inventory falls to the reorder point, determines the optimum number of units to reorder through an economic ordering quantity (EOQ) model, and sends an electronic reorder to the supplier. Such a model ensures that the canned food inventory is maintained at an optimum level while simultaneously minimizing the ordering and holding costs. The model may show that canned tomatoes should be reordered whenever the stock on hand falls below 10 cases and that the optimal reorder quantity is 50 cases at a time. When the stock on hand falls below 10 cases, the information and decision system automatically sends out a reorder to the supplier for another 50 cases of tomatoes. All this activity occurs without any human intervention and is based solely on the data gathered and organized by the information system.

Likewise, for a line department, the initial screening of applicants for entry-level jobs may be relatively routine in some organizations so that it can be moved to an automatic mode. This solution relieves an HR manager from interviewing applicants who do not meet the predetermined screening criteria. Technology even exists to help managers identify the best and brightest from active and passive candidate pools and that counsels senior employees on retirement strategies and options. These technologies allow the HR budget to be directed to tasks where automation is not easily used.

Expert Systems

Expert systems, as the name implies, seek to duplicate the decision process used by an expert who gathers data, organizes it, applies subject matter expertise to interpreting it, and thus makes a decision.

Expert systems can be developed to schedule employees for specific times and days to achieve proper staffing levels or to keep track of a hotel's room inventory to control the maximum yield for each night's inventory of available rooms. The HR department can use expert systems software for career planning. These systems guide clients along the career-planning process by offering expert advice when the system detects a problem in how a manager is developing an employee's career path. They also give nonjudgmental expert advice to managers as they counsel their employees, or to employees seeking guidance independently.

How an HR department sets up the external and internal information systems that organize and disseminate knowledge throughout the organization affects clients' ability to attain their goals. Just as HR must supply clients throughout the organization with adequate information, the same is true for the information provided to the HR staff. By taking the necessary care to determine what is the right information, the right time, and the right presentation format both externally and internally, HR adds tangibility to its delivery of truly client-centric service.

Chapter Takeaways

1. Know the informational needs and expectations of each client and your own HR staff.
2. Evaluate the value and cost of information to each client, making the "right" information available in a format the client will understand and use.
3. Utilize technology in an information system wherever applicable, while retaining the "personal touch" necessary to maintain high-level, client-centric service.
4. Effective information systems accelerate employee empowerment.
5. An HR department cues its client commitment through the content and structure of its information system.

Chapter 8.

Service Delivery Systems: Ensuring Client-Centric Service

"Being nice to people is just 20 percent of providing good customer service. The important part is designing systems that allow you to do the job right the first time."
— Carl Sewell, author, *Customers for Life*

A British Airways baggage handler at London's Heathrow Airport noticed that passengers waiting for their luggage at the carousel were asking him a strange question time and again: "How can I get a yellow and black tag for my bags?" The passengers had noticed that bags with those tags arrived on the carousel first, so they wanted the "special" tags. The baggage handler realized that because the passengers asking him the question were the first ones to arrive at baggage claim, they had to be the first-class passengers who deplaned first. And yet they had to wait 20 minutes on average for their bags, while passengers in coach were getting first-class luggage service. First-class passengers are highly profitable to airlines. Something was clearly wrong with the service being provided to them.

By asking around, the baggage handler discovered that the passengers perhaps least deserving of "first-class" luggage service — those flying on less expensive standby tickets, the last people to board the plane — nevertheless were the first to receive their specially tagged bags. Since they were the last to board, their luggage was loaded last and unloaded first. The baggage handler made a simple suggestion: Load first-class luggage last. Although the idea sounded simple, implementing it meant that the airline had to change its luggage-handling procedures in airports all over the world. Even though that took time, they did it. The average time it took to deliver first-class luggage from the plane to the carousel dropped from 20 minutes to fewer than 10 minutes worldwide, and fewer than seven minutes on many routes. This change occurred because a motivated, observant employee saw a way to improve the system and got it done.

The employee — working for a company that wanted to meet its customers' expectations for quality service, especially for its first-class passengers — saw a chance to improve the service delivery system and jumped on it. The employee had no idea that his simple, conscientious suggestion would lead to a monumental, companywide shift in the way it served its customers. Nor did he guess that he would receive a service award that included two round-trip, first-class tickets to the United States.

A System for Client-Centric Service

Service delivery system design is among the least studied and understood topics in service management. Yet it is a crucial topic. Delivering client-centric service — in short, satisfying clients by meeting or even exceeding their expectations — and avoiding service failures require giving careful attention to the delivery system design. Restaurants know that smiling and pleasant staff or food prepared perfectly with the finest ingredients does not matter if the meals are served cold when they should be hot and served hot when they should be cold. If the delivery system fails, the service fails with it, no matter how many other things are done right. On the other hand, a service delivery system that is not only well designed but adaptable in the ways it can meet the evolving needs of clients goes a long way toward providing the service experience the customer expects. Moreover, a well-designed system will take into account the possibility of failure by building in recovery routines and processes to ameliorate client frustrations when service fails. In short, the delivery system can make or break the service.

The focus of this chapter is on properly designing HR service delivery systems beyond the information system discussed in the prior chapter. Here we focus on the combination of technological processes, organizational systems, and the people who deliver the service to the client. This chapter builds on earlier discussions about creating a client-centric HR strategy and culture, as well as on hiring, training, and motivating staff who can execute a client-centric vision. All these are necessary, yet not sufficient, for ensuring that an HR system works in client-centric ways. Even if your service strategy is defined and your staff are trained and motivated to deliver client-centric service that the client needs, wants, and expects, service excellence will be impossible to attain if the system is poorly designed.

The message here is simple: Study all the parts of your HR delivery system in detail to identify potential failure points; design accurate early warning measures for each of the many failure points; engage the entire HR staff to monitor those measures; and follow up on *everything*. If failures occur repeatedly at certain points, change the system design. Client-centric HR managers keep a careful eye on all the places where an HR system might fail, and they do their best to keep failures from happening. Should a failure occur, they correct the error in the client's favor.

Service Delivery Trilogy

Analyzing a service delivery system has three major steps: *planning, measuring,* and *improving*. In the quality improvement literature, these components are known as "Juran's Trilogy" (or the "quality trilogy"), named after quality-management expert Joseph M. Juran.

Let us take a look at each step of the trilogy in depth.

Service in Action: SAS Group

Consider a motivated, empowered purser at Scandinavian Airlines. A planeload of SAS passengers was stuck at an airport due to snow. Because the purser knew that the SAS philosophy is to do whatever is necessary to satisfy customers, she decided to offer them complimentary coffee and biscuits. She went to the catering supervisor, a middle manager who outranked her, and asked for 40 extra servings. Because only so many cups of coffee and biscuits were allocated for each flight, the catering supervisor, sticking to the rules, refused her request.

The purser could have let the system defeat her. Instead, she noticed that the plane at the next gate belonged to Finnair, an airline that purchased food and drinks from the SAS catering department. The SAS purser asked the Finnair purser to order the coffee and biscuits. The

Planning

Any good delivery system begins with careful planning. A careful analysis and detailing of every step in the entire service delivery process make the difference between having it "mostly right" and reaching the level of excellence that the very best service organizations deliver.

Service standards should be established early in the planning process. They are the quality control metrics when you do not have tangible products to measure with caliper-like precision. Standards define the company's expectations for how the different aspects of the service experience should be delivered every time to every client. For example, as demonstrated in this chapter's opening discussion, airlines define how many minutes it should take for bags to get from the stopped aircraft to the baggage-claim area. If the bags are not on the conveyor belts in the specified time, then the service-quality standard has not been met. Many organizations set a standard number of rings for answering the phone in a customer service response area. If a reservationist, for example, has not picked up the phone within catering supervisor was required by SAS regulations to fill the order. The SAS purser bought the coffee and biscuits from the Finnair purser with petty cash, and the stranded customers received a welcome snack — a thoughtful touch that sent the valuable message that SAS cared about them and appreciated their patience in an unavoidable delay. These are the types of actions that help make a frustrating delay tolerable and, more importantly, build customer loyalty.

The SAS purser solved a problem before the system could fail the clients, finding a way around an ineffective supervisor. Through the actions of one empowered employee, the system avoided a potential failure to achieve the airline's primary goal: customer satisfaction. Everybody was happy — except the bypassed catering supervisor.

three rings, the service quality standard has not been met. These are service quality standards, established during the planning phase, that guide employees in what quality and kind of experience they are expected to deliver to customers.

Service standards are one of the best tools HR managers have to determine that the service expectations of their clients are being met. Standards also establish the basis for the second step, measuring the quality of the client's service experience.

Measurement to Manage

The need for measuring what is happening to a client in every step of the service delivery system is necessary for understanding service delivery problems when they arise, for defining what and where the problems are, and for knowing when the solutions being tried are working. Being prepared to provide feedback to an HR staff member on the level of client service he or she achieved last month is extremely helpful for establishing a client-centric culture in an

HR department. When the service performance measures are clear, attainable, and understood by the staff as to how they relate to service standards, staff members can and will assess themselves, correct their own errors, and even compete with each other to be successful. Self-management through self-measurement is a fundamental premise for the W. Edwards Deming quality-circle movement.

Teaching HR staff what is necessary to be client-centric and then training them to measure how they are performing on those critical factors lay the foundation for a self-managing, client-centric HR staff. The measures should permit employees to monitor their effectiveness while delivering the service. If Sam, an HR staff member, has been told that HR's maximum for answering the phone is three rings, and a computerized device displays a running record of how many rings it takes Sam to answer a call, Sam knows at all times where she stands in relation to the goal.

At a department level, measuring customer satisfaction with existing delivery system performance can identify opportunities for improvement. Recall the earlier discussion in Chapter 1 about "guestology," Disney's term for its study of visitors to its parks and resorts. In a similar way, HR can study the impact of its delivery systems on its line managers and their employees to learn what they need, want, and expect from the HR department.

In an example from the hospitality industry, Marriott's managers at one hotel thought a hotel's surplus funds should be spent on adding small television sets for bathrooms. But the housekeeping department had a different idea: By keeping track of requests for ironing boards, time spent delivering the short supply of ironing boards, and customer complaints when ironing boards were not available, the housekeeping department was able to show management that the funds should be spent on ironing boards instead of on televisions.

Improving the System

The last component of the service trilogy is improvement. Information about what is actually occurring drives system improvement. If you can identify where the system is failing to deliver what a client expects, you can figure out how and where to fix the system. Once the plan is clearly laid out, and the results of implementing that plan are adequately measured to yield insights into how well the system is operating, HR staff will have the information needed to redesign the system to yield continuing improvements in client service.

Often, a big challenge for HR is getting people to self-report failures. While telling a supervisor about a problem created by someone else is easy, telling a supervisor about a problem you created is hard. This issue is a vital one to resolve because people on the front line are often the first to notice system failures, and frequently they are the reason the failure occurred. If they have been properly motivated to report failures, especially those they created, they will willingly report failures, knowing that this information can contribute to system improvement. Employees must be praised for telling others about their errors. Doing so creates a "learning organization."

The Continuous Cycle

The cycle of planning, measurement for control, and continuous ongoing improvement never stops. Client-centric HR departments
1. plan what the HR service delivery system should be doing,
2. measure whether what is planned is in fact happening, and
3. improve continuously.

Its commitment to this process focuses everyone's attention on detecting, analyzing, and solving problems in delivering the HR product to its clients.

Thus, the design for a service delivery system must incorporate all three stages. A good plan includes creating a measure of how well the plan is implemented at every step of the service delivery process and how the overall plan is succeeding. These measures allow the recording of "exceptions" to the plan and trigger an

Service in Action: The Ritz-Carlton

Horst Schulze, former chief operating officer of the Ritz-Carlton Hotels, tells the story about how one hotel manager solved the problem of room service breakfasts arriving late. After several customers complained about their breakfasts — they were arriving too slowly and were cold, as well — the manager knew it was time to investigate. The traditional managerial solution to the problem would have been to call in the offending room service manager and criticize that person for technical incompetence and poor supervisory skills. This properly disciplined manager would then return to the kitchen, gather the room service staff around, and chastise them. In most organizations, blame rolls downhill.

Instead, the manager decided to ask the employees who were affected by the problem to solve it. He organized a team of room service people and asked them to study the problem, find out why the meals were not getting to customers within a reasonable time, and suggest ways to solve whatever problem they found. Surprisingly, the team discovered that the cause was the unavailability of elevators needed by the room service staff to deliver the meals quickly to their customers. They then studied why the elevators were so slow and even had a room service employee spend an entire morning in an elevator with a stopwatch to track all the elevators' movements and to see what they were being used for and why they were not available when the room service staff needed them.

What the employees found astonished Schulze. The problem was traced to a faulty management decision about how many bed sheets each floor was allowed to stock (called the "par") for the housekeepers. The decision had left some floors with too few sheets. Consequently, the housekeepers used the elevators to hunt for extra sheets to finish cleaning the rooms on their floors. As a result, the elevators were unavailable to the room service delivery staff when they needed them. Hot meals were delivered late and cold. Because a manager trying to save on the cost of sheets had stocked too few, the rest of the system was disrupted. This seeming cost-saving move drove up the costs of room service (because the hotel did not charge for meals when customers complained) and housekeeping labor (because housekeepers were spending their time in elevators instead of making beds). Trying to solve a problem in one part of the service delivery system had created problems for another part. The result was an increase in costs and, worse, an uptick in customer dissatisfaction.

Who would have guessed that the problem of late breakfasts could be solved by adding more bed sheets to the available supply on each floor? Schulze drew three lessons from this story. First, managers do not always have the time or information to figure out the best solutions to all their problems by themselves. Therefore, they tend to pounce on the simplest, quickest conclusion — namely that a subordinate is not sufficiently motivated, trained, or supervised. Such managers rely on the erroneous assumption that "if you correct the person, you correct the problem." Second, employees are often in the best position of finding the root cause of a problem that affects their work. The most advanced information system or technological analysis would not likely have uncovered this problem, whereas the people doing the job did.

Finally, the most valuable lesson is that every problem should be addressed from the perspective of the entire service delivery system, with regard to the organizational issues, as well as to the technological processes.

We can even put this idea in the context of the total quality management (TQM) movement. TQM emphasizes that everyone is responsible for quality. When a service failure occurs, HR managers should seek problems in the system before blaming employees. As Schulze noted, you can have all the characteristics and features of a high-quality hotel, but the system can still fail from time to time. His goal was to include all hotel staff in the system design team to create what he terms a "self-healing system" in which employees are empowered to override the system to fix customer problems. Also as important, the hotel's employees are responsible for telling management when and where a system has failed so that together they can fix it. Just as all employees are responsible for providing and maintaining quality, they are also responsible for finding and fixing service failures and, when failures occur, to fix the system.

analysis of those exceptions to the rule, or variations from the plan. A well-designed system includes a way to identify and measure every critical part of a client's experience. You cannot fix something you do not know is broken. A plan includes the measures that enable a delivery system to be controlled and, when broken, fixed.

Most people respond to their experience "as a whole." They are often unable to identify how any one part of their experience influenced the determination of their overall satisfaction. They are simply left with an impression of service quality. A restaurant customer, for example, may be unhappy with the dining experience at a restaurant. Until management carefully analyzes the data by measuring each step in the entire customer experience, management is unlikely to recognize that the customer's dissatisfaction was not caused by the server or the food but by a dirty bathroom, or a messy entrance littered with cigarette butts. Knowing the system thoroughly and having the appropriate measures to judge its effectiveness trigger the necessary corrective actions. Client-centric HR managers seek to measure everything HR does in order to guarantee their clients get what they need from HR. They measure formally through surveys and informally through client inquiries and discussions. They do so constantly and consistently so that the HR department does what the organization needs it to do to support its managers and employees.

Assigning Accountability

Management consultant Karl Albrecht likes to tell a story about showing a group of hospital managers how the cycle of service appears from the point of view of the patient. After defining all the tasks necessary for delivering the hospital services needed by patients, one manager suddenly said, "But no one is in charge." In other words, because of the way the traditional hospital is organized, no one person is responsible for making sure that service is smooth, seamless, and most importantly, focused on the patient. Each department and every function had a manager, but no one in particular was responsible for being certain that all the subservices worked together for a patient's benefit. The same manager elaborated on this point:

"Our hospital is organized and managed by professional specialty — by functions like nursing, housekeeping, security, pharmacy, and so on. As a result, no single person or group is really accountable for the overall success and quality of the patient's experience. The orderlies are accountable for a part of the experience, the nurses for another, the lab technicians for another, and so on. There are a lot of people accountable for a part of the service cycle but no one has personal accountability for an entire cycle of service."

Service in Action: The Ritz-Carlton

While discussing how The Ritz-Carlton Hotels won the Malcolm Baldrige Quality Award, Horst Schulze told about finding a cross-functional organizational solution to identify and correct system flaws. The Ritz-Carlton had used customer surveys to identify 18 chief customer-satisfaction measures. Senior management hired a process manager for each hotel whose responsibility was to eliminate flaws and reduce work-cycle times by 50 percent in the systems that delivered the 18 keys leading to customer satisfaction. These keys were considered so essential that this specific person was tasked with confirming that someone focused on them all the time. The Ritz-Carlton avoided the drawbacks of a functional orientation that haunt so many large organizations. It did this by authorizing the process manager to cross all functional areas to make certain that someone was focused on satisfying the hotel's customers.

Similarly, Janet N. Parker, the Executive Vice President of Corporate Human Resources for Regions Financial Corporation, reports her experience with one of her bank's clients:

"A firm wanted to shift from being U.S.-centric to becoming a global organization so as to increase its relevance for its members. Progress in this undertaking proved to be extremely slow. When the board investigated the reasons for the glacial movement, it discovered the problem was due to departments in the organization showing more concern for protecting their respective turfs than for attaining the organization's goals. Marketing, branding, external affairs, public affairs, and government relations were spread all over with no clear champion. Consequently, critical issues for becoming global were ignored or appeased."

An axiom of the late management guru Peter Drucker had been forgotten by these functional leaders: "Employees must work for the good of the organization — not a division, department, or functional group."

The lesson here is clear: A client-centric HR department needs to use an organizational design that enables every HR service product and all HR staff to focus on the client in an integrative way. While an organization chart typically shows functional units with different people responsible for different things, all HR staff should know that their real boss are their clients, both as individuals and as the overall organization.

Chapter Takeaways

1. A badly designed service delivery system can ruin the reputation of a client-centric HR department.
2. A service delivery system is made up of three parts: *planning, measuring, and improving.*

3. Check for system failure before blaming people, and whenever possible, put employees to work to analyze and solve delivery problems.

4. Detailed planning can minimize most service failures and provide for a quick recovery.

5. Problems should be addressed holistically from the perspective of the entire service delivery system.

6. Everyone in HR is responsible for monitoring and maintaining the quality of the service delivery system.

Chapter 9.

Becoming a Valued Member of the Senior Management Team

"If you can't get it for yourself, who's going to get it for you?"
— Fritz Perls, father of Gestalt Psychology

When Jack Welch addressed the Rotman School of Management at the University of Toronto, he asked the audience who they thought had been the most valuable person on his team. When one MBA student hollered, "the CFO," Welch responded in mock indignation that with a Ph.D. in chemistry, he did not need someone to tell him how to add or subtract. When a second MBA student shouted with exuberance "the marketing manager," Welch became equally indignant when he responded jokingly that the student was looking at the greatest marketing as well as salesperson in GE's history. After several more guesses from other students who all but worshiped finance — at this point you could have heard a pin drop in the audience — Welch finally gave his answer: "My HR manager." Why the HR manager? Because only the HR manager, Welch explained, knows how to grow individuals and create winning teams. One of the authors of this book, Gary Latham, has a framed sheet of paper on the wall in his office that reads: "HR is King," signed by Jack himself.

How did Welch's HR manager gain such a prominent seat at the policy table? HR staff members had proven how HR could add value to GE's success through its client-centric practices. More importantly, once they got to the table, HR's continuing commitment to serving clients and its demonstrated success in helping clients achieve their goals kept them there.

Throughout this book we have focused on how HR can adopt client-centric practices and actions from the service industry to help clients attain their goals. When HR approaches its job with a client-centric philosophy, it enhances the likelihood that it is doing, and is seen as doing, invaluable work for the organization. How smart you are does not matter if no one ever asks you for your advice. Whom do you listen to or seek out when you need advice? People who demonstrate that they want to help you succeed, or people who show that they are only interested in doing their job and do not truly care about your ability to reach your goals? Client-centric HR staff convince clients throughout the organization that HR is there to help them be more effective than they would be otherwise.

We have presented a number of ways to be client-centric in previous chapters. In this chapter, we explain why a client-centric focus is valued and how to sustain that perception of value by clients. Winning someone's respect and trust is one thing; sustaining that respect and trust is something else. We turn therefore to the methods of (1) achieving successful co-production of HR services with clients and (2) improving clients' ability to deliver HR expertise to their respective teams.

Fostering Client Co-Production

People do not go to a cafeteria expecting a server to offer them a menu, to McDonald's expecting white linen table service, or to Southwest Airlines expecting a desk agent to check them into a flight. People know that when they go to a cafeteria, they will help themselves to what they will eat, that when they go to McDonald's they will likely stand in line to order food and, after eating, dispose of their trash, and that when flying Southwest, they will check themselves in at the next available check-in kiosk. Most people are used to doing things for themselves to get the service they expect. HR service does not need to be different. Indeed when clients co-produce HR services, they can get what they need in the way they want it.

The first step in successful HR co-production is to identify which HR services clients want to perform for themselves. If a client wants a great deal of control over hiring decisions, for example, a client-centric HR department should ask that client, "What can we do to help?" If a line manager says she wants HR to send the resumes of only the top 10 candidates and to help identify the ones who best fit the department's culture, that will be a different degree of co-production from the line manager who wants HR staff to screen and hire for the open position. Different clients want different levels of responsibility. A client-centric HR manager finds out what a client wants and needs and then works to ensure that the client helps co-create the solution to that need. Both managers above will likely be delighted with the HR department if the person hired is a good fit, even though they requested varying types of assistance from HR. A key to HR's success is to ask clients what they want and then to determine how HR can help them be successful by involving them in co-producing their solutions.

Benefits to HR

Co-producing a service benefits both the client and HR staff. First, co-production allows a client to get what is wanted in the way it is needed. HR service is often an idea, an approach, or a way of doing something (tacit knowledge). Clients typically have their minds set on how a given service should be delivered. This service is rarely available in the form of a standard software package, instructions in a handbook, or the standard operating procedures (SOPs) of an HR department. Client-centric HR departments start every client contact with the idea that the client will be co-producing HR services; HR staff members must figure out how they can co-create value with the client by enabling them to co-produce it. This approach presents a new way for an HR department to look at clients, viewing them as co-creators of HR services.

Managing human resources (as compared to the HR department)

is the responsibility of everyone in the organization. This is true regardless of title or job role. Yet, HR clients must often learn how to co-produce with HR its products, services, and procedures. Client-centric HR departments accept the responsibility to co-produce successfully. Involving clients in co-producing HR tasks requires HR staff to acquire the skills and ability to successfully collaborate on HR policies, procedures, and services with its clients. The good news is that involving clients is worth it because it improves the clients' service experience.

In the service industry, co-production has long been a mantra. Some think of co-production as "self-service," but it is much more than that. Simple examples of co-production include salad bars in restaurants, coffee makers in hotel rooms, automatic teller machines, online product ordering, and self-serve gas pumps. Services provided by HR that can and should involve co-production with clients include job analysis, hiring, performance management, and training. Client-centric HR considers every service desired by a client as co-produced and approaches the client with the attitude that together we will co-create solutions to your problems and attain your goals.

Advantages to Clients

The advantages of co-production for HR clients are at least fourfold. First, co-creation decreases the opportunity for an HR service failure because it increases the perception of HR service quality in the eyes of clients. Since clients define the value and quality of HR, co-production increases the likelihood that clients will see HR practices as relevant and valuable. Co-producing HR solutions enables clients to get what they want with the quality and value they want. If clients are co-producing hiring decisions, they can hardly fault HR when the person does not work out; they got the employee they chose. Moreover, co-producing solutions provides HR the opportunity to win the respect and trust of clients. When client-centric HR staff develop ways to help clients make wise decisions, they establish themselves as valued partners.

Second, co-production improves time management. The customer who chooses to use the ATM instead of going inside the bank to stand in line to see a teller saves time. Fast-food restaurants make their reputation and define their market niche on the basis of saving time for their customers. In HR, co-production with clients in developing the content and delivery of training programs keeps the content relevant to a client's goals. In addition, co-production gives a client the capability to deliver the training when and where it is wanted.

Third, co-production reduces the risk of unpleasant surprises for clients. If a diner's customers walk through a cafeteria buffet line, they see exactly what the food products are, instead of ordering off a menu and hoping for the best. Involving clients in setting HR's goals, and the strategies and actions for attaining them, helps clients obtain what they need and want from the HR department to be successful in attaining their own goals. If a client, for example, has a new union contract to implement, co-producing the language and components of that contract with the HR labor negotiator will eliminate any surprises or unknowns in the terms of contract language.

Fourth, if clients co-produce HR services, the service will be designed with the client's abilities, needs, capabilities, and goals in mind.

HR must carefully specify the predetermined sequence of operations when co-producing HR services that solve client problems. More importantly, HR staff must take responsibility for guiding clients to successfully co-produce these HR outcomes. This is because a client who encounters obstacles or setbacks while co-producing an HR service is likely to give up on the system and, by extension, on the HR department. Not only must HR develop its own mastery of its services and the delivery of those services, it must develop the client's mastery of them as well. This process of enactive mastery, or building client efficacy, will be discussed in greater detail below.

Restaurant owners know that signs in a self-serve cafeteria must indicate clearly the entry point; the location of the trays, silverware, and napkins; and how the customer is to proceed through the food selection and payment stations. Cafeteria workers must be alert to spotting confused-looking people wandering around looking for signs, directions, and instructions on how to participate successfully in this food delivery process. Similarly, HR staff must be ready, willing, and able to help a client be successful in co-producing an HR service. Additionally, HR staff must be alert to possible failure points in any HR process or procedure that a client has co-produced. The process for line managers to follow, for example, when disciplinary action is warranted, in accordance with the union contract must be made sufficiently clear by HR for the managers to navigate without incurring a grievance.

When Does Co-Producing Make Sense?

Co-production makes sense when it frees HR for other tasks, reduces client waiting time, increases efficiency and effectiveness, and builds client commitment. Each of these is discussed further below.

Freeing HR for Other Tasks

Co-production reduces the costs of hiring HR staff to do what clients can do for themselves. The more clients do for themselves, the fewer staff HR needs on payroll. In addition, client co-production allows HR to draw upon the expertise of managers and their employees. If managers are encouraged to take primary responsibility for one or more HR services, the HR staff is freed to handle more elaborate or complicated HR tasks. In an example from the hospitality industry, patrons at many Epcot restaurants are allowed to make their own reservations by touch-screen television or online. Consequently, hosts and hostesses take very few routine reservation phone calls. This technological solution permits them to spend more time responding to the needs of customers who request complex information or advice. Thus, the quality of the restaurant service increases with no increase in costs.

In a similar fashion, the strategy of offering a buffet at lunch is an effective way for restaurants to stay open at lunchtime without over-extending their servers. Many servers are unhappy working at lunchtime because the checks and, hence, tips are relatively low. In addition, employees tired from working at lunch are less likely to work efficiently at the dinner hour. A buffet provides meals with minimal use of waitstaff, the customer gets a good price on the meal, the restaurant provides a better work situation for its servers, and the service in the evening is better than it would have been if servers had also worked at lunchtime.

Co-Producing Reduces Waiting

By definition, value is added by reducing costs for the same quality, increasing quality for the same costs, or both. Costs include those incurred by choosing to co-produce with HR staff instead of a client performing the function solo. For example, if a potential customer sees a long line outside her favorite restaurant, the time/cost of waiting for the next available table may be viewed as so great that she willingly goes to a nearby fast-food restaurant to minimize the time/cost of getting a meal. The customer may experience a decrease in quality but expects a greater decrease in overall cost that will compensate for it.

Similarly, line managers want to be sure that HR's service quality is at least equal to what they would get if they did it themselves before seeking the help and support of HR staff. Those clients who can co-produce HR services with a client-centric HR department derive value from knowing that they are getting service "their way." Home Depot has made a lot of money serving customers who believe they can enhance the quality and value of their home repair by doing it themselves. But Home Depot works hard to keep customers who do the work themselves from failing. Customers look to Home Depot to take the necessary steps to see that they do the work correctly.

HR clients who co-produce HR services minimize the risk that an HR staff member will not provide them the service they want. Many people now search the Internet looking for the best value in both hotel accommodations and flight reservations. By doing so, they take responsibility for co-producing the travel experience they want, without involving a travel agent who may push packages that are more in the agent's interest than in theirs. In a similar way, an HR department that helps clients co-produce HR experiences can show how an HR service enables them to attain their goals.

Efficiency and Effectiveness

Involving clients in the development and enhancement of HR

Service in Action: IT Services

Steve Jarrett, former senior Vice President of Human Resources for the Financial Industry Regulatory Authority and a former SHRM Board member, gave an example of co-production at a large IT services company. When management decided to broaden the career opportunities of its high-performing sales and consulting employees, it faced an interesting challenge. The challenge was not just finding ways to mitigate the negative impact on sales as a result of removing these high performers from the field; the challenge was also to lessen the negative reactions to a decrease in compensation for these employees since they would not be on a sales incentive system while performing the training. Employees who were to be moved out of field positions, even for a short period of time, would receive standard compensation plans that would significantly decrease their earning potential. Because of this decrease, these high-potential, revenue-generating employees, who had initially shown the desire to become general managers, chose to forego this developmental opportunity. Their refusal hurt their ability to services can increase the department's efficiency and effectiveness. If a restaurant offers a buffet at lunch, it has the opportunity to derive income from its physical plant and food-production capacity without overusing its human resources. A hotel offers automated check-in and check-out for customers who do not want to wait in line. A rental-car agency offers automated check-in and check-out service for its "best" customers. In these ways, service organizations maintain a constant staffing level while still being able to accommodate variability in customer demand.

Building Commitment

Arguably the most compelling reason for co-production of HR services is to build ongoing rapport with clients. When clients discover that HR staff respects them, their goals, and their

be considered for even bigger roles in the organization, and it hurt the organization's efforts to develop its "bench strength."

By working with the business lines, benchmarking other practices, and soliciting input from these employees, the sales people co-produced a solution with HR. The new salary plan included an employee's base, plus a percentage of the potential compensation the employee would receive as part of the leveraged plan to create a special payment. This special payment minimized the gap between the leveraged and standard compensation plans. Because these employee developmental assignments were for only 18 to 24 months, an employee received this special payment at the beginning of each leg of an assignment. While this co-produced payment plan did not completely close the compensation gap, it was a significant improvement. Consequently, most employees chose to participate in the career development program. The employees were appreciative that their concerns had been heard, and HR was proud that it had involved its client in devising a creative fix to a sizeable challenge.

expertise so much that they are wanted as partners in co-producing HR services, they are likely to become supporters of the HR department. Co-production is a straightforward way to get clients to take ownership of HR staff, products, systems, and procedures.

Creating Successful Co-Producers

As is true for any job position that needs to be filled, a client-centric HR department must ask the following questions about its clients as co-producers: What are the knowledge, skills, and abilities (KSAs) necessary for clients to co-produce HR services? What is the motivation of HR clients to co-produce HR services? How can HR appeal to that motivation? Does HR have the KSAs necessary to train clients how to co-produce HR services? Will clients use their HR skills if HR staff spends the time and money to train them? If the answers to these questions are positive, the expenditure of the HR department's time and money will be worthwhile.

Benchmark service organizations take steps to manage the confusion and uncertainty customers can create. They typically do so by thinking of their customers as quasi-employees and by "managing" them accordingly. This approach means designing HR service products, the environment, and the delivery systems to take advantage of the KSAs of their clients. Similarly, a client-centric HR department that sees its clients as partners in co-producing HR services seeks to design its systems to accommodate the KSAs of its clients.

Professors Ben Schneider and David Bowen, organizational psychologists, proposed a three-step strategy for treating customers as quasi-employees that can be adapted by HR departments to use when attempting to engage their clients in co-producing HR services:

1. Involve your clients in the analysis of jobs to define the KSAs required for them to interact effectively and efficiently with HR staff.

Service in Action: A Globally Diversified Company

Co-production of international assignments had gone awry at a globally diversified company: Frustrated line managers were assigning people they no longer wanted as employees or people nearing the end of their careers to international postings. A Senior Vice President of HR found a solution that involved the co-production of line managers.

He recognized that the true cost of a failed international assignment to the company far exceeded what the clients perceived. He needed to get managers to appreciate how much it truly cost the company in terms of salary differentials, tax accommodations, travel, housing, and so forth when it sent an engineer overseas. By his calculations even an $80,000-a-year engineer cost the company over a half-million dollars for a two-year assignment. Steps needed to be taken by HR and clients to make sure that the person given an international assignment would not fail. A failure would not only cost the half-million dollars, it would disrupt the rest of the organization because failed expats had to be replaced, new domestic jobs had to be created, and so forth. The solution was to transfer the costs of expats from HR to the operating units, so they would see the impact of these costs to their bottom lines. When HR shouldered the costs, the clients were oblivious to the consequences of failed expats. When the budget responsibility was transferred to them, line managers immediately realized their part in co-producing expat assignments more efficiently and effectively.

2. Ensure that clients have the proper training to co-produce HR services.

3. Assess a client's ability and willingness to co-produce HR tasks effectively. In effect, conduct a performance appraisal of all clients to verify that the experience being co-produced with HR is meeting their and your expectations. If it is not, identify what needs to be modified. Does a client need further training? Is something about the service setting or delivery system impeding a client's effectiveness in accomplishing HR-related tasks?

In short, client-centric HR staff must help clients succeed as co-producers because the risk of failure is always present. If a dude ranch allows inexperienced riders to go off alone on horseback, the result could be humiliation or broken bones, not to mention a lawsuit. Similarly, HR must tactfully intervene to keep clients from failing, let alone from putting the entire organization at risk. HR staff must recognize when to intervene before a failure occurs. The staff must do so with sufficient tact so that a client is not embarrassed (for example, making a job offer to an unqualified friend of the family). Many clients fail to appreciate the cost of performing HR tasks incorrectly, as illustrated in the above example of the global company. Educating and overseeing clients so that they co-produce HR functions right is a major responsibility for HR.

Evidence-Based Client Co-Production

Even when clients have the ability to perform an HR service, they are likely to fail if they lack the confidence in their ability to succeed. Large numbers of studies by Stanford University psychology professor Albert Bandura show that ability is necessary but not sufficient for performing effectively. It is what we tell ourselves about our ability that matters more. If we say, "we can't," we will not do well in spite of high aptitude. Further, one severe failure or multiple small ones can spiral into learned helplessness. On the other hand, as clients become more confident in their ability to do a task, they become more optimistic about their ability to co-produce the same and similar HR tasks successfully in the future. Thus, HR must make certain that it not only provides the necessary training and skill sets for clients but also instills in them a strong belief that they will succeed in co-producing an HR service.

Knowing how to co-produce an HR service is not enough; clients must believe they can do so effectively. All the training and education in the world cannot help clients who do not believe in their capability to master a task. Bandura's research shows us that "If you think you cannot, you cannot." Thus, the first step in successful co-production is to assure a client's ability (by training), and the second step is instilling high self-efficacy (a belief in the ability to succeed). The inclusion of client ability and self-efficacy in the co-production process illustrates a critical difference between claiming to be a client-centric HR department and actually being one. If you as an HR manager do not include a plan for developing self-efficacy in the department's co-production process, you will diminish HR's chances of being successful. When you watch equally talented partners in a tennis doubles match where one obviously does not believe in her ability to win, you can confidently predict who will lose. Likewise, when a client does not believe he will succeed in co-producing an HR service, not only will he fail to do so, but he will attribute his failure to an incompetent HR department. Thus, HR must place equal emphasis on developing a client's ability and self-efficacy.

Self-efficacy is a person's conviction that "I can cause," "I can bring about," or "I can make happen" — in short, the sense that "I can do this." Clients who have strong self-efficacy set and commit to high goals. When they experience setbacks, they persist until solutions are found. Clients with low self-efficacy are quick to abandon a goal as soon as they encounter difficulties (for example,

"I can't do this. Give it back to HR and let them do it!").

A client's self-efficacy is determined in one or more of four ways: enactive mastery, modeling, persuasion by a significant other, and self-talk. Clients, before attempting to co-produce an HR-related task, will ask themselves if they have done something like this before and, if so, how did it work out? A person will also look at others to see how those she considers similar to her in talent and ability succeeded when performing this task. Additionally, a client will pay close attention to the opinions of others the client respects, responding to expressions of encouragement or discouragement regarding the client's likelihood of performing effectively. Finally, a person will look in the proverbial mirror to see if he feels ready to do something. Jumping off a bridge — even with a bungee cord — is a very frightening experience for first timers. They hear the words of encouragement or discouragement from their friends; they watch when others they perceive as similar to them jump successfully or unsuccessfully; and they pay attention to their own self-talk as they encourage or discourage themselves. If all the steps of this decision process build self-efficacy, they jump. If the steps lead in the other direction, they will not. Once they jump successfully, they know they can likely do it again well. Producing a "can do" co-producer is a function of one or more of these four factors coming together in one person for one task at one time. Self-efficacy is task-specific confidence in success.

Creating this "can do" belief on the part of clients begins with training on how to perform the task. This process is called enactive mastery. If this HR task is similar to a previous co-production experience, remind the client of the points of similarity. This reminder promotes confidence: "I can do this!" Divide the task into subtasks. Sequence the tasks in ways that all but guarantee success. Small wins instill task-specific confidence for future tasks. Just as a server must oversee customers cooking their own food at a fondue restaurant without letting them fail, HR must oversee their clients co-produce HR experiences to prevent failure.

Once one client has successfully done what is required to co-produce a succession planning program or any other HR service, that client may be used as a model for encouraging other clients to try it. Moreover, when many clients successfully co-produce an HR service, they are not only models, but they become cheerleaders for others to try it. Knowing that peers have tried and succeeded at an HR task makes it more likely that the remaining line managers will give it a try too. After all, "If they can do it well, so can I!" The only caveat for HR is to find a model with whom the client identifies.

A third way to increase self-efficacy is by persuasion from a significant other — an individual we respect and listen to closely. We tend to behave in accordance with the expectations of those who are meaningful to us. Consequently, this person can help or hinder a client in instilling confidence to co-produce a task. The job of HR staff is to keep eyes and ears open to identify a significant other for a given client in the workplace. Once you find a client's significant other, ask that person to talk to the client and encourage him by letting him know why he is likely to perform well in a co-production with HR.

Finally, HR can use visualization and self-talk as a way to build clients' belief that they will be successful if they co-produce HR services. Just as Olympic runners close their eyes and envision ways of winning a race, HR can teach clients to visualize a successfully co-produced HR service. HR staff can also teach functional self-talk to increase the likelihood of success. A successful coaching session, job interview, or disciplinary session are areas for putting envisioning to good use. The bottom line is simple. If clients believe they will fail in co-producing the HR service, they most likely will. Conversely, if they believe they will succeed, they most likely will. Thus, client-centric HR staff members play a role in co-production by taking responsibility for promoting success in the co-production experience by building client self-efficacy for co-producing HR services.

Self-efficacy is important to develop in HR staff as well. Telling stories in HR meetings or highlighting HR successes in organizational publications are effective ways to reinforce the belief in the staff that they too can succeed. Likewise, exposing HR staff to organizations that are benchmarks of successful client-centric co-production instills a belief in your HR staff that they can do what the very best HR staff do. At team meetings, let those who are successful tell how they succeeded, so that those who are still unsure can listen and learn. Spreading stories of self-efficacy among staff is another strategy for building a "can do" mindset.

Chapter Takeaways

1. Engage and motivate clients in co-producing as much of their HR service experience as is possible and practical.
2. Identify and develop KSAs of clients to enable them to co-produce HR services.
3. Train HR staff in ways to achieve successful client co-production, including self-efficacy techniques.
4. Boost HR staff and client self-efficacy to foster all-around excellent performance.

Chapter 10.
Sustaining HR's Value to the Top Management Team: HR Managers as Service Leaders

"The most valuable 'currency' of any organization is the initiative and creativity of its members. Every leader has the solemn moral responsibility to develop these to the maximum in all his people. This is the leader's highest priority."
— W. Edwards Deming, author, *Out of the Crises*

"Servant-leadership is all about making the goals clear and then rolling your sleeves up and doing whatever it takes to help people win. In that situation, they don't work for you, you work for them."
— Ken Blanchard, author, *The One Minute Manager*

Throughout this book we have described a path to becoming a valued member of the top management team by transforming HR into a client-centric department. By focusing on the needs, wants, and capabilities of HR's clients, the HR department can identify what it can do to best help them attain their goals. By applying the lessons of the best service organizations, the client-centric HR staff can ensure that clients will see HR as a department that truly serves their needs by co-producing solutions to the many human resource challenges they face. By transforming itself into the service leader, HR can earn its place at the top management discussions on the most critical resources the organization has – its human resources. By also becoming the servant leader, HR sustains its place at the table.

Robert Greenleaf developed the notion of servant leadership on the basis of what helped him be successful in his own experiences as a leader at AT&T. Although the idea of servant leadership was originally articulated for line managers, we close this book by drawing a connection between this widely known concept and service leadership. Throughout this book we have emphasized service industry principles that can be readily adapted and applied to HR management. Our service leadership principles parallel servant leadership because the principles underlying it are so similar to what we have advocated in the preceding chapters. The bottom line of both concepts is that trustworthiness and authenticity are the foundations of leadership. Line managers and their employees care less about how much the HR staff knows until they understand how much HR cares about helping them attain their business objectives.

A fundamental principle of service leadership is that it starts with HR's efforts to gain an in-depth knowledge of its clients and their needs, wants, capabilities, and goals. When the HR department makes a commitment to truly learn the client's agenda and to put it first, ahead of its own, trust is earned and authenticity established. Learning what the client needs, wants, and expects from HR and then putting these first is the commitment to service we have written about throughout this book. This commitment to providing individualized client-based service is the basis of service leadership. The line manager complaint that HR is typically pushing its own agenda without any thought given to client needs is a reminder of a bygone era. Today's HR service leader is uniquely concerned with the success of each client. Service leadership creates an HR culture that ensures HR staff act in the best interest of each client and ends manipulative self-serving behavior.

So how does one become a service leader? The research indicates that these leaders share at least six characteristics:

1. *Listening*: A deaf ear equates to a closed mind. Listening gains knowledge. Truly listening establishes the trust that builds and sustains enduring relationships with HR's clients.

2. *Empathy*: Service leaders take active steps to know the needs, wants, capabilities, and goals of each line and staff manager, and they appreciate that each client has something uniquely valuable to contribute to the organization.

3. *Awareness*: HR service leaders must be cognizant of the organizational culture, especially moral and ethical norms and values. This knowledge enables an HR manager to ascertain conflicts of interests and find common ground.

4. *Persuasion*: The ability to convince a client to take action without relying on coercion or formal positional power is a fundamental skill required of an HR service leader.

5. *Stewardship*: A service leader takes responsibility for the success or failure of the HR organization, particularly the HR issues that impact the organization as a whole.

6. *Commitment to the growth and empowerment of people*: An HR service leader allocates resources to the growth and empowerment of others. This process includes helping people learn from their failures in addition to their successes. A service leader helps create a culture that brings out the best in people.

The theme underlying these principles of service leadership is that the role of the HR manager can no longer be defined by the traditional leader-follower relationship. Today's HR leadership role is instead that of a client-server. Thus, client-centric HR managers view themselves as stewards who are entrusted with the responsibility of not only attracting, developing, and retaining the organization's human resources, but also enabling the successful achievement of their goals. Client-centric HR managers are, and are seen as, trustworthy and authentic service leaders dedicated to enhancing the needs, capabilities, and goals of each member of the workforce.

Researchers have found that servant leadership fosters a service culture in an organization. Building on the research on servant leaders, the principles we presented in this book can lead to success for HR in today's organizations. One survey of 1,500 firms, for example, found that those that were committed to servant leadership had improved employee retention, increased productivity, and elevated the company's market value. Servant leaders mold a service culture by (1) imbuing service values in the HR staff (for example, personal integrity, building relationships, helping clients grow and develop) and (2) accentuating policies, practices, and procedures that reinforce service behavior. Since servant and service leadership parallel one another, we extend the research findings on servant leadership to service leadership. Thus, service leadership, like servant leadership, offers the best path for HR departments to gain client trust by showing authentic commitment to empowering today's workforce.

So where do we end this book? The best place to end is with a message that rephrases, in service leadership terms, two key client-centric ideas from Chapter 1 — focus on the client, and value each and every client. The message is simple and complex, profound and obvious, easy to write and difficult to do: To transform an HR department into a service leader role requires a commitment to serving others in a leadership role. Only by building and sustaining a service culture for HR can this transformation occur. Hiring, training, and motivating the right people are necessary but insufficient conditions for service leadership. The HR leader must walk the service walk and talk the service talk to create a service culture that guides every HR staff member to consistently and constantly practice service values and to display a service mission. Doing these things well enables the "new HR" to be seen as a respected partner by line managers. The existence of HR service options external to the organization prohibit the HR department from ignoring the fact that its true competitive advantage is service — service to the organization and to its employees.

When line managers and their employees see HR practicing the principles of service leadership with every client every day, they will quickly see the value of including HR at the decision-making table when organizational policy is made and strategy determined. Transforming HR to a service leadership role will encourage others in the organization to solicit, hear, and value HR's input. Being invited to participate in policy decision-making is a challenge that many HR departments have yet to overcome. An organization's human capital is important today and will likely be even more so tomorrow. HR departments must show their value to the organization by demonstrating effective paths clients can follow to build high-performance teams that internalize and accelerate the implementation of an organization's strategy with excellence. The surest way to gain and keep client trust and respect is to show through its client-centric actions how HR can help clients co-create and co-produce the HR activities that lead to goal attainment.

Endnotes

The embedded examples were collected by the authors from written responses to questions posed to the various people cited. They are generally acknowledged at the front of the book, but we thank them again here for taking the time to provide these rich illustrations of transforming HR.

The hospitality examples used are generally from Robert Ford, Michael Sturman, and Cherrill Heaton, 2012. *Managing Quality Service in Hospitality*. Albany, NY: Delmar.

Other examples where referenced to their respective sources can be found in the following:

Brinker: Norman Brinker and Donald T. Phillips. 1996. *On the Brink: The Life and Leadership of Norman Brinker*. Arlington, TX: Summit Publishing Group.

Four Seasons: Isadore Sharp. 2009. *Four Seasons: The Story of a Business Philosophy*. New York: Penguin Group.

Marriott: J. W. Marriott, Jr. and Kathy Ann Brown. 1997. *The Spirit to Serve: Marriott's Way*. New York: Harper Business.

Scandinavian Airlines: Jan Carlzon. 1987. *Moments of Truth*. New York: Ballinger.

Southwest Airlines: Kevin Freiberg and Jackie Freiberg. 1996. *Nuts! Southwest Airlines' Crazy Recipe for Business and Personal*

Success. Austin, Texas: Bard Press; see also, J. H. Gittell. 2005. *The Southwest Airlines Way: Using the Power of Relationships to Achieve High Performance.* New York, McGraw-Hill.

The Ritz-Carlton: J. Michelli. 2008. *The New Gold Standard: 5 Leadership Principles for Creating a Legendary Customer Experience Courtesy of the Ritz-Carlton Hotel Company.* New York: McGraw-Hill; see also Leonardo Inghilleri, Micah Solomon, and Horst Schulze. 2010, *Exceptional Service, Exceptional Profit: The Secrets of Building a Five-Star Customer Service Organization.* New York: AMACOM.

Walt Disney Company: Stephen M. Fjellman. 1992. *Vinyl Leaves: Walt Disney World and America.* Boulder, CO: Westview Press. *Walt Disney: Famous Quotes.* 1994. Printed for Walt Disney Theme Parks and Resorts; David Koenig. 1994. *Mouse Tales: A Behind-the-Ears Look at Disneyland.* Irvine, CA: Bonaventure Press; Jane Kuenz, S. Willis, and S. Waldrep (eds). 1995. *Inside the Mouse: Work and Play at Disney World.* Durham, NC: Duke University Press; Bill Capodagli and Lynn Jackson. 2006. *The Disney Way, Revised Edition: Harnessing the Management Secrets of Disney in Your Company.* New York: McGraw-Hill; Tom Connellan, 1997. *Inside the Magic Kingdom : Seven Keys to Disney's Success.* New York: Bard Press; Lee Cockerell. 2008. *Creating Magic: 10 Common Sense Leadership Strategies from a Life at Disney.* New York: Crown Business.

Wendy's: Dave Thomas. 1992. *Dave's Way.* New York: Berkeley Books.

For more on strategic planning and forecasting tools see any of the many strategy texts, such as R. D. Ireland, R. E. Hoskinson, and M. A. Hitt. 2008. *Understanding Business Strategy,* 2nd ed. Cincinnati, Ohio, South-western; A. A. Thompson and A. J. Strickland. 2008. *Strategic Management,* 14th edition. McGraw-Hill, New York; or R. C. Ford, M. C. Sturman, and C. P. Heaton. 2012. *Managing Quality Service in Hospitality.* Albany, NY: Delmar.

For more on servant leadership see Robert Greenleaf. 1997. *Servant Leadership*. Mahwah, NJ: Paulist Press or Ken Blanchard. 2003. Servant Leadership. Nashville, TN: Thomas Nelson. For those seeking more academic work on this topic, see S. Sendjaya and James Sarros. 2002. Servant leadership: its origins, development, and application in organizations, *Journal of Leadership and Organizational Studies*, 9, 57-64; C. Brewer. 2010. Servant leadership; A review of the literature. *Online Journal of Workforce Education and Development*, IV, 1-8; F. Walumba, C, Hartnell, and A. Oke. 2010. Servant leadership, procedural justice climate, service climate, employee attitudes, and organizational citizenship behaviour: A cross level investigation, *Journal of Applied Psychology*, 95, 517-529; D. van Dierendonck (2011). Servant leadership: A review and synthesis, *Journal of Management* 37, 1228-1261.

For classic writings in services with rich examples, see the following:
K. Albrecht. 1988. *At America's Service: How Your Company Can Join the Customer Service Revolution*. New York: Warner Books.
Leonard L. Berry. 1995. *On Great Service: A Framework for Action*. New York: The Free Press; see also, L.L. Berry and K. Seltman. 2008. Management Lessons from Mayo Clinic: Inside One of the World's Most Admired Service Organizations, New York: McGraw-Hill.
T. E. Deal and M. K. Key. 1998. *Corporate Celebration*. San Francisco: Berrett-Koehler.
T. Scott Gross. 1991. *Positively Outrageous Service: How to Delight and Astound Your Customers and Win Them for Life*. New York: Warner Books.
J. L. Heskett, W. E. Sasser, and C. W. Hart. 1990. *Service Breakthroughs: Changing the Rules of the Game*. New York: The Free Press.
B. J. Pine and J. H. Gilmore. 1988. Welcome to the Experience Economy. *Harvard Business Review* 66(4), 97–105.

Carl Sewell and P. Brown. 1990. Customers for Life. New York: Pocket Books.

Ben Schneider and David Bowen. 1995. *Winning the Service Game.* Cambridge, MA: Harvard Business Press.

Index

Page numbers followed by b, t, or f indicate box features, tables, or figures, respectively.

Additional SHRM-Published Books

Becoming the Evidence-Based Manager:
Making the Science of Management Work for You
By Gary P. Latham

Business-Focused HR: 11 Processes to Drive Results
By Scott P. Mondore, Shane S. Douthitt, and
Marisa A. Carson

The Chief HR Officer: Defining the New Role of Human
Resource Leaders
Edited by Patrick M. Wright, John W. Boudreau,
David A. Pace, Elizabeth "Libby" Sartain, Paul McKinnon,
and Richard L. Antoine

The Cultural Fit Factor: Creating an Employment Brand
That Attracts, Retains, and Repels the Right Employees
By Lizz Pellet

Got a Minute? The 9 Lessons Every HR Professional Must
Learn to Be Successful
By Dale J. Dwyer and Sheri A. Caldwell

HR Competencies: Mastery at the Intersection of People and Business
By Dave Ulrich, Wayne Brockbank, Dani Johnson, Kurt Sandholtz, and Jon Younger

Human Resource Essentials: Your Guide to Starting and Running the HR Function
By Lin Grensing-Pophal

Never Get Lost Again: Navigating Your HR Career
By Nancy E. Glube and Phyllis G. Hartman

The Power of Stay Interviews for Engagement and Retention
By Richard P. Finnegan

Proving the Value of HR: How and Why to Measure ROI
By Jack J. Phillips and Patricia Pulliam Phillips

Reinventing Talent Management:
How to Maximize Performance in the New Marketplace
By William A. Schiemann

Rethinking Retention in Good Times and Bad:
Breakthrough Ideas for Keeping Your Best Workers
By Richard P. Finnegan